Discovering GOD'S DESIGN

A Journey to Restore Biblical Womanhood

Amanda Walker

WESTBOW
PRESS®
A DIVISION OF THOMAS NELSON
& ZONDERVAN

WestBow Press books may be ordered through booksellers or by contacting:

WestBow Press
A Division of Thomas Nelson & Zondervan
1663 Liberty Drive
Bloomington, IN 47403
www.westbowpress.com
1 (866) 928-1240

ISBN: 978-1-5127-1192-9 (sc)
ISBN: 978-1-5127-1193-6 (hc)
ISBN: 978-1-5127-1194-3 (e)

Library of Congress Control Number: 2015914641

Print information available on the last page.

WestBow Press rev. date: 11/23/2015

Lovingly Dedicated:
To my husband, Chris

You have been a constant source of love,
support, and encouragement. Thank you for not
allowing me to give up and seeing this project
through to completion. What a fun and exciting
journey we have been on these last few years!
I love you!

To my precious children, Makaylan Joy,
Hannah Elizabeth, and Aaron Christopher

May you grow to be godly men and women
who love and serve Jesus with every breath.
My prayer is that I model to you the definition
of a biblical woman. Mommy loves you!

To my mentor, friend, and professor, Terri Stovall

Thank you for giving me the idea/push to
write this study and then believing God
could accomplish it through me. You are
a blessing to my life and ministry!

So God created man in His own image;
He created him in the image of God;
He created them male and female.
Genesis 1:27

Contents

Introduction

Biblical womanhood. This phrase tends to evoke images of a quiet, timid, and submissive woman who is skilled in cooking, sewing, crafting, and mothering. Let me take a wild guess: in your mind, a biblical woman *is* the Proverbs 31 woman. And you have given up on ever being her. In all honesty, you are not even sure you want to attempt to emulate her. (Actually, you may be thinking, "she seems quite boring.") If this describes your view of a biblical woman, then welcome! You are not alone.

My journey to understanding biblical womanhood began fifteen years ago. I was getting ready to graduate from college, and many of my friends were getting married. Attending wedding after wedding and seeing the joy on my friends' faces as they married the man of their dreams was priceless. (What woman doesn't like a good love story?) Inevitably, the pastor began reciting the wedding vows. He turned to the woman and asked, "Do you promise to love, cherish, submit, and cleave to your husband?" At that point, the hair on the back of my neck bristled. I looked forward to the day I would love a man—but submit to a man—not on your life! I prided myself in being independent, strong, and capable of handling life on my own. A man who had the last word in a discussion or decision was not appealing. I was comforted in discovering that submission was a thing of the past, and Jesus' death and resurrection "liberated" women from the role of submission. However, slowly but surely, God began to challenge my newfound freedom.

After graduating from college, I spent two years overseas working with the International Mission Board. My team leaders were a married couple who took it upon themselves to disciple the eight young singles under them. Their marriage had a rhythm that I had not witnessed before. The wife was a strong, outspoken, independent, and educated woman who knew her convictions and stood up for them. However, she also adored her family and submitted to her husband. Her husband was just as impressive. He was a strong, distinguished, and biblically educated man—but he was not intimidated by his wife's strong personality. Instead, he led her, and she followed him. For the first time in my life, I began to wonder if I had misunderstood the biblical meaning of submission and womanhood.

After my overseas assignment, I returned and immediately enrolled in seminary. The goal was to get a counseling degree with the intention of adequately counseling and discipling others. However, God had a different plan. Two weeks into the semester, I dropped two of my counseling classes and enrolled in a women's studies class titled A Biblical Theology of Womanhood. To say the class infuriated me would be an understatement! Every Tuesday and Thursday I endured my professor and her teaching as she explained the biblical roles of men and women within society, the church, and the home. How could this highly educated woman proclaim: "The highest calling of a woman is to be a wife and a mother"? I was neither married nor a mother, so I must have missed the "high calling!" (This was said with seething sarcasm.) Throughout that semester—with me kicking and screaming—God began to slowly reveal the sinfulness of my rebellious heart and the truth hidden within—*I was a feminist and did not know it.*

In my quest for independence and individualism, I lost sight of what it meant to be a Christ follower. In the process, I refused to surrender my womanhood to God. Without a heart of surrender, understanding God's purpose for authority and submitting one's life to His authority is impossible. It was refreshing to learn that submission to God's authority didn't mean He wanted to stifle the person or personality He created in me, nor did God call me to be a "doormat" for others to walk over. I can be an independent, strong, sometimes stubborn, educated woman *and* also be obedient to God's pattern for womanhood. (Praise the Lord for that!)

Biblical womanhood is not about conforming to a particular personality type. Instead, biblical womanhood is about conforming to God's design for womanhood. (After all, He is the One who made us.) My prayer is that God would use *Discovering God's Design* to help you in your journey toward understanding who you are as a woman and to discover how God wants to use you in His kingdom. If you are at the beginning of this journey and the words *submission, roles,* and *authority* sound like bad words, then I am glad you are here. (Well … at least you are considering being "here.") I pray my journey will challenge and encourage you to move forward and discover all that God has for you. At times, you will probably get angry with me and want to throw the book across the room. After you give the book a good lob, go over, pick it back up, and continue the journey. You will not be sorry. However, you may be one who rarely struggles with submission and authority, and I am so glad you joined me. We can learn much from your example. Prayerfully, this study will help you press on in your journey as a woman and encourage you to stay the course.

I do not want this to be a one-sided journey. My intention is that you would interact with the material and take your own journey to restoring biblical womanhood. Therefore, the material is designed as a six week study. I did not break each week into five days, so please feel free to do it all in one sitting or in small clumps throughout the week. I have provided some natural breaks to help those who want to digest the material in small bites.

There are also main questions titled "Rest Stop" scattered throughout the study. So, pay close attention and resist the urge to hurry past them. Instead, stop, soak in the question, and then respond. I am confident that God will show you great truths hidden in your very own journey. Never forget that God desires to use every woman—regardless of her personality and background—to be a powerful force in His kingdom. I am glad you are on this journey with me. Let's get started!

Week 1

THE JOURNEY BEGINS:
UNDERSTANDING GOD'S DESIGN

Defining the Terms

Have you ever walked into a conversation and realized you had no clue what people were saying? You knew they were speaking English, but you didn't understand the context or meaning of the words. This situation happens to me every fall and spring semester. My husband is the college pastor at our church, and our local university is known for its outstanding engineering program. When I see a new student, my first question normally is, "What do you study?" Half the time, the answer includes one of the engineering programs. Being a glutton for punishment, my follow-up question is, "I would love to hear about your program. What would your degree allow you to do?" And just like that, I've opened Pandora's box. The student begins a monologue on their particular program using such terms as *nanotechnology, thermodynamics,* and *stress analysis.* They are talking, but all I hear is *blah, blah, engineering, blah, blah, blah* … As soon as my eyes begin to glaze over, my husband comes to the rescue. Gently fading into the background, I shake the cobwebs from my brain and seek out other less intimidating conversations.

Have you ever been in a conversation like the one described? If so, how did you respond?

Sometimes theological terms can seem like those engineering words. Knowing how to spell them can be a daunting task—have you seen how long they are?—so understanding their meaning appears impossible. However, they are important. I want to introduce you to common terms used in discussing the theology of biblical womanhood. I use them throughout the Bible study, so I want you to know them and be able to say and spell them. This section may seem a little tedious, but hang in there. I promise you, you will be glad you did.

Biblical Theology of Womanhood

Let's get right to it. I have already used the term *biblical theology of womanhood* several times, and you may be wondering what in the world I mean. Understanding its meaning is not as difficult as it appears. The easiest way to define a biblical theology of womanhood is to break down the phrase into its individual words.

Biblical—The word *biblical* means "according to the Bible." Anything that is described as *biblical* means it has its origins (a beginning) and meaning in the Bible.

ᔆᘇ ᘓᔆ

*A biblical theology of **womanhood** is defined as* **"what the Bible (from Genesis to Revelation) says about women and their position in the family and the church."**

ᔆᘇ ᘓᔆ

Theology—Theology is simply "the study or science of God."[1] When you study theology, you actually study the Bible to see what God has revealed about Himself. Beware of people claiming

2

that they have developed a "new theology" based on human reasoning or pop psychology. As we continue our journey, you will see how educated and sincere teachers mishandle Scripture to make it fit their view. Every Bible teacher is vulnerable to the misuse of Scripture. Our goal is to let Scripture speak for itself and base our theology on what Scripture—not society or the culture—says.

Womanhood—*Womanhood* means "what distinguishes a woman from a man." Womanhood can also mean "things that pertain to being a woman."

Therefore, a biblical theology of womanhood is defined as "what the Bible (from Genesis to Revelation) says about women and their position in the family and the church." See, it wasn't that difficult. Are you ready for a few more?

Created Order

I will also use the term *created order* when speaking about womanhood. However, the created order is much easier to explain than define. In its simplest definition, the created order refers to the fact that God created man (Adam) first and then created woman (Eve) out of man. You may be thinking, *So what's so important about that?* Well, I'm glad you asked. The created order has *everything* to do with gender roles and responsibilities in a marriage and in the church order. As we dig deeper into Genesis 1–2, you will discover that God uses the created order as the blueprint for the male and female gender roles in a marriage relationship. We will also find that the New Testament writers refer back to the created order when giving instructions on church order (1 Cor. 11:1–12 and 1 Tim. 2:9–14). So when you hear me appeal to or mention the created order, your ears should perk up and your mind should immediately go back to the beginning of creation.

Egalitarian (Evangelical Feminist) Position on Womanhood

The egalitarian/evangelical-feminist view of womanhood is one of two theological camps that explain and define womanhood. Before we define it, please note that *egalitarian* and *evangelical feminist* will be used interchangeably. So don't get confused when you see me flip back and forth between these terms.

The egalitarian position is hinged on one verse in Scripture. (At this point, there should be a blaring warning signal going off in your spirit. Basing a position on one verse is a theological no-no!) The verse is: "There is no Jew or Greek, slave or free, male or female; for you are all one in Christ Jesus" (Gal. 3:28). Based on Galatians 3:28, egalitarians believe gender roles within the family and the church are a result of the fall of Adam and Eve in Genesis 3, and differing gender roles were not part of the created order. Therefore, Jesus' death and resurrection restored men and women back to a place of equality, which means that men and women do *not* have different roles in the family and the church.[2]

To be fair, evangelical feminists do not dismiss the Old and New Testaments. In fact, egalitarians have a high view of the Bible and agree that Scripture is authoritative (holds authority) and is without error. It is the Scripture's teaching on gender roles that gives them problems. Using the ancient historical context of Scripture—this simply means the culture and norms of people in the ancient world—or the fall of man in Genesis 3, egalitarians easily explain away the Bible's usage of traditional gender roles.

At the beginning of my journey, I was an evangelical feminist. (However, I didn't know such a term existed.) Therefore, I understand this view and can identify with you who realize this is where you are. My prayer is that over the course of our study, God will begin to show you His truth from Scripture about gender roles.

In your own words, define the egalitarian (evangelical feminist) position of womanhood.

Complementarian Position on Womanhood

The complementarian position developed as a response to the rapid growth of feminism within the church. (Take a quick poll of your church friends and you will discover that feminist views are just as popular in Christian circles as they are in society.) However, unlike the egalitarian position, complementarians do not have one specific verse they use to define their position. Instead, they use the whole counsel of God's Word to explain and justify their position.

ഇ ൝

Men and women are cut from the same mold, but we are different with differing roles and functions.

ഇ ൝

The *complementarian position on womanhood* states that God created man and woman equal in their worth and standing before Him (Gen. 1:27), but He has given them different roles in their relationship to one another (Gen. 2:15, 18; Eph. 5:22–33).[3] That is the theological definition, but the everyday English definition is a little easier to understand: men and women are cut from the same mold, but we are made different with differing roles and functions.

I have two preschool daughters, and they already know they are not like their boy cousins. In fact, my oldest says, "I am a girl, and girls like flowers, bunnies, and kitty cats." Believe me, I didn't have to teach her that (I'm not a fan of cats, and I'm more of an athletic—not prissy—girl). My prayer is that you will come to realize that the fall of man and woman (Gen. 3) did not make us different. God *created* man and woman different. Now that is something to celebrate!

REST STOP: Think back to your home life and ministry. Which theological position of womanhood is consistent with your daily actions? (Notice, I did not ask which one you believe is described in Scripture.)

I am going to challenge us to reexamine our view of womanhood in light of Scripture, and some of those truths are going to go against every fiber of our natural flesh. Are you willing to allow God and His Word define your theology? If so, write a prayer asking God for His wisdom and help as you seek to be obedient to His Word.

We Are Image-Bearers

I will never forget the first glance I had of my firstborn's sweet face. She was an absolute miracle. Never in my life had I seen someone so beautiful—this momma's heart was overwhelmed with love, joy, and excitement. I studied every inch of her tiny body. She had my nose, my husband's dimple on her chin, my feet, my husband's hands, and definitely my personality (her strong-willed personality shone from the beginning). She was perfect! Did you know that God felt the same way when He made the first man and woman? Let's read about it.

If you have children, what was it like when you first laid eyes on your precious little one?

The Design: Man and Woman Created in God's Image

Read Genesis 1:26–28 and Genesis 2:7–25.

In these verses we get to see God in His role as skillful designer. God only needed to speak, and the earth, heavens, sun, moon, stars, vegetation, and animals came into being. He spoke one last time: "Let Us make man in Our image"—and the world would never be the same.

In order to understand the incredible creative power of our heavenly Father, we must take a deeper look at the original meaning for the word "created." In Genesis 1:27, the Hebrew word for "created" is the word *bara*. The word *bara* means "make from nothing." This word is used in Genesis 1:1, 21, and 27, and it always signifies something new is about to occur.[4] In using the term *bara*, God, through Moses, is saying, "Listen up! I am about to do something that has never been done before.

I have just made the heavens, earth, animals, and now I am about to create something completely different. I am making a new creation ... man." I love this portion of Scripture. The entire chapter is leading up to this moment—the creation of humanity.

Genesis 2:22, uses another Hebrew word for "made"—*bana*. *Bana* is translated "builder, fashioned, made." While *bara* shows God's power to speak things into being, *bana* depicts the personal involvement God had with His new creation.[5] In a sense, God was willing to get His hands dirty in the forming of humanity. Isaiah 64:8 says that God is the "potter" and we are the "clay." What a beautiful imagery of God's love for His unique creation! He could have spoken us into being, as He did with the rest of creation. Instead, God stooped down, took a clump of dirt, formed the dirt into what looked like man, and then leaned over and breathed into his nostrils the breath of life (Gen. 2:7). Then, God caused a deep sleep to come over Adam. While Adam slept, God was busy forming and crafting Eve to be Adam's helpmate (Gen. 2:20–22). Just thinking about God's intricate attention to detail in creating us overwhelms me. Listen to how one commentator described Genesis 2:20–22:

> That the woman was made of a rib out of the side of Adam; not made out of his head to rule over him, nor out of his feet to be trampled upon by him, but out of his side to be equal with him, under his arm to be protected, and near his heart to be beloved. ... In this (as in many other things) *Adam was a figure of him that was to come; for out of the side of Christ, the second Adam, his spouse the church was formed,* when he slept the sleep, the deep sleep, of death upon the cross, in order to which his side was opened, and there came out blood and water, blood to purchase his church and water to purify it to himself.[6] (Emphasis added)

Wow! Isn't it amazing that God, the Holy One, Ancient of Days, the Almighty Father, cares so much for us—His special creation—that He took the time to form us out of the dust of the ground? Please hear your Creator shout to you: I LOVE YOU! YOU ARE VALUABLE TO ME! I HAVE A SPECIAL PLAN AND PURPOSE FOR YOU!

What are some emotions or thoughts that stir within your spirit as you consider that God took time to build and form you?

The Difference: We Were Designed as Male *or* Female

When you see a pregnant mother, what is one of the first questions you ask (or at least want to ask) her? You want to know whether she is having a boy or a girl. Genesis 1:27 is very clear: God made humans either male or female. The American media and culture tells us that one's maleness or femaleness is a product of our conditioning and surrounding, and your gender has nothing to do with God's design. However, something (Someone) within us says that there is a fundamental difference between men and women. If you are a woman, then God made you a woman. He is not surprised at your gender, and He did not make a mistake. You,

୫୦ ଓୡ

If you are a woman, then God made you a woman. He is not surprised at your gender, and He did not make a mistake. You, like me, may be described as a "tomboy" or athletic, but God still created you to be a woman with a softness and femininity that is not present in men.

୫୦ ଓୡ

like me, may be described as a "tomboy" or athletic, but God still created you to be a woman with a softness and femininity that is not present in men.

I have seen this distinction when my nephews come over to play. My three nephews tend to be a little more aggressive. Anything can become a makeshift sword, and they love cars, balls, and dirt. However, my daughters are a little gentler. My oldest daughter dresses up in every princess costume she owns and forces her boy cousins to play the prince. My youngest walks around with an armful of baby dolls, and sword fights have never been an issue in our home. Yes, it is true that many little girls enjoy playing outside in the dirt, like my youngest daughter, and some little boys like baby dolls—but the way boys and girls see the world is different. God, in His creative wisdom, designed them this way. Furthermore, God, in His wisdom, designed you to be you. So, whether you are a "tomboy" or a beauty queen, embrace your womanhood and relish in God's design of you.

If you have been around children, have you seen a difference in the way little boys and little girls act? If so, how?

Are you more of a "tomboy" or a beauty queen? How have your personality and preferences affected you as a woman?

THE ASSIGNMENT

The Designation of Roles for Men and Women

You may be thinking, "We didn't make it through the first chapter without her mentioning the roles of men and women!" I don't want to lose you here, so before we discuss those assignments, I want to clear up a few misunderstandings on gender roles. First, I will *not* say that a man should be a lazy, absent husband and father who sits in front of the TV and doesn't help his wife with the daily maintenance of their home or the discipline of their children. As a mother of two preschoolers, I need my husband's help. Secondly, I will *not* say that it is sinful for a woman to work outside the home. Though Scripture clearly teaches that God has given women the *primary* role of taking care of their family and being the manager of their home, this pursuit—for some women—may involve work outside of the home. However, a woman must take extreme caution that her work doesn't come at the expense of her first priority—her family and her home. Lastly, I will *not* say that a man is superior to a woman or that a woman is superior to a man. So, what *does* the Bible have to say about the roles of men and women within the family? Let's find out.

Shared Responsibility

Genesis 1:28 says, "God blessed them, and God said to them, "Be fruitful, multiply, fill the earth, and subdue it. Rule the fish of the sea, the birds of the sky, and every creature that crawls on the earth."

Based on this verse, what are the two roles men and women share?

If you answered "have babies" and "rule over creation," then you are correct. Go on and pat yourself on the back.

Procreation

First, God commands man and woman to have children. Since my husband is a college pastor, I get to disciple young women on a weekly basis. Almost every week, one of them asks me about being a wife and mother. They eventually want children, but they fear children will be a hindrance to their marriage or career. I understand their fears. Being a mother is an enormous responsibility and a task that shouldn't be entered into lightly. But, God has given married couples a command: "be fruitful, multiply, [and] fill the earth." For those of you who are married, this truth leads me to respectfully ask you a question: Are you, if God allows, willing to be a mother, or do you use every means of birth control to prevent pregnancy? For fear that you may misunderstand me, this command isn't about the dos or don'ts of birth control. Some women are advised, for various reasons, to avoid pregnancy. Therefore, I do not look down upon any of you who have chosen this path. But I can't help but wonder why we try so hard to prevent life when God is the Giver of life. My prayer is that we would begin to see the importance of bearing and caring for children and learn how that mirrors the heart of God.

I also don't want you to hear me say that having children is the *only* way to please God. I didn't get married until I was almost thirty-one, and I had my first child at thirty-two. So, I understand that the command to procreate isn't just about how many children you have but the *view* you have toward children. You may have eight or nine children, yet consider them a burden and a hindrance to your life. You may have no children but consider children worthy of respect and desire to mentor and disciple the children and teenagers who are in your life. Ladies, God made us to be mothers—whether physical mothers or spiritual mothers—to those He brings into our lives. Let's take this responsibility seriously.

I have a few questions for you to consider. If you are married, are you seeking to be obedient to this command? Maybe the harder question is: Do you view children—even your children—as a hindrance and burden to you, or as a gift and blessing from God?

If you aren't married, what is your view toward children?

Before we move to the next point, I want you to spend some time praying over how you view children and specifically the command to bear children. If you have bought into the lie that children will stifle your marriage or your career, are you open to what God wants to do within your family? You may be missing out on the biggest blessing of your life.

Rule over Creation

God also gave men and women the responsibility to rule over all living things. With power comes responsibility. First, we have the responsibility to make sure we take care of the earth. When you go to any major city or drive along the interstate, there are miles and miles of trash littering the streets. Christians should be the frontrunners in teaching society how to take care of the environment. Second, we are given the task to rule over creation and not allow creation to rule over us. "Go Green" is a common phrase in our culture. While it is important to take care of the earth, God has also given plants and animals as resources to use and as food for us to eat.[7] As Christians, we must be careful to be good stewards of God's earth, but we must also be careful to not allow ourselves to worship the creation which God has given us authority over.

Differing Responsibilities

Take a moment and reread Genesis 2:7–25. Before we move on, I want you to consider some questions about this passage.

Do these responsibilities come before or after sin entered the world?

Do Adam and Eve seem content or irritated with their responsibilities?

Our human nature is bent toward becoming defensive against anything we don't understand, so please resist the urge to close the book and run for the hills. As I tell my students, hear me out and then give me your response. I think you will be pleasantly surprised.

Man as Provider

Let's first look at the man's responsibilities. The first task given to the man is for him to be the primary provider and protector of his family. In Genesis 2:15, God tells Adam to work and watch over the Garden of Eden. I want you to notice something—man's responsibility to work was not a result of sin. Ladies, God made man to work and to find fulfillment in his work. I have seen this desire to work play out in my marriage. After we got married, I was working full time and my husband was finishing up his master's program. During those six months, I watched as my husband became more and more frustrated and even resentful of my job. We knew this working arrangement was temporary, but Chris began to feel useless and self-conscious because I was the one working while he stayed home, did homework, cooked, and even cleaned the house. At that time, and for good reason, our roles were reversed, and my husband's confidence suffered for it. That time in our marriage taught me one valuable lesson: my husband (and your husband) was created to provide for me.

Man as Protector

God also gave man the responsibility to "watch over" the garden. The phrase "watch over" is the Hebrew word *shamar*. *Shamar* can also be translated "to keep, watch, preserve, attend, defend, guard, [and] watchman."[8] It is used elsewhere in Scripture to describe a shepherd taking care of his flock (Gen. 30:30–31) or God protecting His children from harm (Gen. 28:15; Exod. 23:20; 1 Sam. 2:9).[9] Ladies, men have a natural desire to protect the people they love. However, in recent decades, culture and the media have portrayed men as weak and women as strong. You've seen it, so you know what I am talking about. TV shows like *Alias* and *Scandal* and movies like

Salt, Charlie's Angels, and *The Hunger Games* depict women as the protector and—at times—the aggressor. Even Disney has traded in their damsels in distress for more aggressive heroines. Disney's *Brave* depicts a little girl who wants to grow up to be a warrior instead of a woman who is married and allows a man to protect her. Yes, we live in a dangerous world where women need to learn self-defense—my husband even bought me a gun so I can protect myself and our girls while he is away—but women must also be careful to not become so independent and self-reliant that they do not allow the men, especially their husband, to protect them.

Some of you may be asking yourself: If a man is to be the provider and protector of his family, is it sinful for a woman to work outside the home? Here's the short answer—*no*. I realize that every family has different needs and not all situations are the same. Some of you are single mothers, and you have to work in order to provide for your children. Even the Proverbs 31 woman is an example of a woman who had some outside business experience. She was capable of buying a field and even sold some of her handmade clothing to help her family financially (Prov. 31:24). But if you read the passage carefully, you see a woman who respects her husband, cares for her household, and submits to her husband's leadership. Any career or ambition that comes before your family and their needs should be questioned. The American culture tells us that we can have it all—a husband, children, *and* a successful career. Yet, women tend to be more stressed, more confused, and less content than they were fifty years ago when mothers were still the primary caretakers of their family. Ladies, God has given man an innate desire to provide for and protect his family, and the woman in his life should allow him to fulfill his God-given responsibility.

REST STOP: If you are married, are you allowing your husband to be the provider and protector of your family? This question is not about whether or not both of you work outside the home. Instead, it is a matter of principle. Do you encourage and then thank your husband for providing and protecting you, or do you seek to be self-reliant and independent?

Man as the Authority

The third responsibility given to Adam was to name all the living creatures, including the woman (Gen. 2:19–20, 23). Imagine the scene with me. After creating Adam, God called all the animals to parade in front of him to see what Adam would name them. I can see him saying, "That animal is fierce and strong, so I will name him 'lion' and his mate 'lioness.' That creature is annoying and buzzes around my head, so I will call it 'mosquito.'" Animal after animal marched in front of him. But, something was missing. What was it? It seemed as if every creature had a mate except him. Out of all the animals, there wasn't a creature that looked like him or was capable of responding to him. So God took care of the problem. God allowed a deep sleep to fall over him. While Adam slept, God took one of his ribs and formed woman (Gen. 2:21–22). After Adam woke up from his God-ordained surgery and saw the beautiful creature standing in front of him, he exclaimed: "This one, at last, is bone of my bone and flesh of my flesh; this one will be called 'woman,' for she was taken from man" (Gen. 2:23). This is the ancient way of saying, "*Wow!* She is absolutely gorgeous!" Adam had finally seen his match, and he was taken aback by her beauty.

You may be thinking, "This is a neat story, but what does Adam naming the animals have to do with me as a woman?" Great question! In the ancient world, the naming of anything showed one's authority over something or someone. Complementarians teach that since God gave man the responsibility to name woman, that action shows his authority over her.[10] Stay with me here … I'm not saying that a man's authority over his wife means that he has permission to dominate her, nor does it mean she is unequal to him. God never intended for a husband to dominate his wife. That is called abuse. Instead, naming of woman implies that God *already* determined that Adam would bear the responsibility to lead his wife. Adam was given the responsibility to protect and lead her, not dominate her.

Egalitarians teach that man's naming of woman had nothing to do with authority. Evangelical feminists admit the man has control over the animals (Gen. 1:28), but that does not stem from man naming the animals. They do not see a need for man to have leadership over his wife because they are both given the command to rule over all living creatures. Evangelical feminists don't differentiate between equal in nature but different in roles.[11] Why? In order to be equal, they must be the same.

This ancient concept of naming and authority may be new to you. What are your thoughts on it? Do you see and understand the rationale, or does it bother you (or both)? I would love to hear your responses.

Man as Spiritual Leader

There is one more responsibility given to the man. God calls man to be the spiritual leader of his family. Though this task is not emphatically stated in Genesis 2, it is implied.

I have a question for you: In speaking with the serpent in Genesis 3, how did Eve know what God told Adam regarding the tree of the knowledge of good and evil? (Remember: She wasn't present when God gave Adam the command.)

If you guessed, "Adam had to tell her," then you are correct.

For Christian men—and arguably all men—the fear of failure is one of the greatest struggles they face. In 2009, Beth Moore was preparing to write her book *So Long Insecurity: You've Been a Bad Friend to Us*. On her blog she asked men to respond to several questions, one which was to define their greatest insecurities. One of the top answers given was a fear of failure, which included whether or not they could effectively lead their families as God asked of them.[12] Ladies, if you are married to a believing husband who desires to lead you and your family, I pray you realize that you have the power to help and encourage your man or the power to deflate his desire to be obedient to this enormous task. If your husband isn't the spiritual leader you want him to be, then begin praying for him ... now. Don't undermine him or belittle his efforts—and certainly resist the temptation to compare him to another man. Instead, I encourage you to move out of the way and let him have opportunities to lead. When he does step up (however small the step) take note and encourage him to continue. If your husband isn't a Christian, then first pray for his salvation, and follow his leadership in other matters. First Corinthians 7:13–14 says that you could be a catalyst for bringing him to faith in

Christ. (We will talk more about that in chapter 3.) We must not forget that, in giving man the responsibility to lead his family, God put upon man the great task of spiritually protecting his wife. It is up to us to help him fulfill that role.

Woman as Helper

There was one responsibility given to the woman. Woman was created to be the helpmate of the man. Being your husband's *helpmate* has nothing to do with being inferior to him or insignificant in God's kingdom. God did not form you to be your husband's servant or doormat, instead God formed you to be a person who could rightly communicate and, in a sense, complete him. (The infamous line "You complete me" from the movie *Jerry McGuire* is running through my mind.)

In 2001–2003, I lived in Taiwan and studied Chinese. If I learned anything in language study it's that there are certain words and phrases that don't easily translate from one language to another. The Hebrew language is no exception. Genesis 2:18 says, "Then the LORD God said, 'It is not good for the man to be alone. I will make a helper as his complement.'" *Ēzer kenegdo* is translated "helper as his complement." The word "helper" is the Hebrew word *ēzer*, which speaks to Eve's role as Adam's helpmate. The Hebrew word *kenegdo* means "corresponding to what is in front of him," which speaks to the fact that both Adam and Eve were equal in their standing before God because they both bear His image.[13] So, why is this phrase so important to our study on womanhood? Because it shows the need man has for woman. The animals could not be the type of helper and companion that Adam needed because they were not like him. (A dog may be described as "man's best friend," but I don't know of a man who has all his needs met by his beloved canine.) Man needs someone who is his equal. A man also needs someone he can adequately communicate with and who will be his companion and helper in life. Ladies, in God's design, we are that helpmate.

REST STOP: If you are married, list two ways you can be a helpmate to your husband this week. It can be practical (like cooking dinner) or emotional (as in having a meaningful conversation).

As stated earlier, please don't confuse "helper" as synonymous with inferior. If you make that mistake, then you will miss out on a very important truth about God and how—on occasion—He relates to His creation. In fact, to equate "helper" as inferior is to claim that God is inferior to man.

Read Psalm 54:4. How does this verse describe God?

In case you were wondering, Psalms 54:4 and Genesis 2:18 use the same Hebrew word for "helper." One is used to describe the woman's role and the other is used to describe God's. So, is God subordinate or inferior to His creation? Absolutely not! God, at times, takes on the role of One who helps His children. This example also plays out in marriage. There are times when my husband takes on the role of helper, especially if I am sick or really need his help with our girls. But, that doesn't negate my primary responsibility as his helper or his responsibility to be the leader of our family.

How has God helped you in your life? Has that increased or decreased your love and need of Him?

Well, we have come to the end of our first week together. We have covered a large amount of material, and I'm so proud of you for finishing. Thank you for persevering and hanging in there with me—at times it wasn't easy. Ladies, God has so much to show us as we continue our journey together. My prayer is that you have come to understand the beautiful design and the creative genius of our God. God doesn't do anything by accident. As we move forward in this journey, rest in knowing that God has a perfect plan and purpose in creating men and women different and giving us differing tasks to complete. Let's delight in and not run from His divine design.

THE DETOUR: WHAT WENT WRONG?

My family and friends will tell you that I am directionally challenged. It doesn't take much for me to get lost or get off track. (My husband even jokes that I get lost going to my own bathroom.) A few months ago, I was traveling to my best friend's wedding. You can only imagine the anticipation I had as I made the eighteen-hour trip from Louisiana to Nebraska. Several hours into the trip I was doing well. The music was blaring, the coffee was hot, and I hadn't gotten lost. And then I saw it—"Hwy 167 detour here." (I could see that a construction crew was working on a bridge, so they made the traffic go another route.) I traded my four-lane highway for a curvy, two-laned, tree-filled back road. I could no longer relax and sing to the top of my lungs. Instead, I had to concentrate on the road, look out for crossing deer, and pray that I didn't miss my sign that the detour was over. Adam and Eve also experienced a detour from their peaceful life in the garden.

Last week we left Adam and Eve in the Garden of Eden. They were in love and enjoying the beautiful garden and relishing in their intimate relationship with their Creator. And then something went terribly wrong.

THE CONVERSATION THAT LED TO SIN

Before we get started, let's read Genesis 3 in its entirety, and then we'll take it section by section. If you have ever started a read-through-the-Bible plan, then I'm sure you have gotten this far. However, I want you to slow down; read every word; and let yourself feel the suspense. To help you, I want you to answer the following questions:

Who did the serpent approach?

Who was originally given the command to not eat of the tree of the knowledge of good and evil?

How did Eve know that she was not to eat from the tree?

Who was with her when she ate of the fruit? (Hint: see v. 6.)

In that moment, what responsibility did Adam abdicate?

Before we talk about the theological implications of this one chapter, I want to point out the obvious. What woman stands around and talks to snakes? I'm thinking God would have used another animal to get my attention, because I would have turned and run for my life. OK … now that's over. Let's look at what happened—and the cost—of that one conversation.

A Talking Snake and a Deceived Woman

Scripture says Satan (disguised as a serpent) approached Eve and asked her one simple question: "Did God really say, 'You can't eat from any tree in the garden?'" (Gen. 3:1) Look back at the actual command in Genesis 2:16–17.

What does God actually say in Genesis 2:16–17?

Satan takes delight in taking God's Word and twisting it. He started with Eve, and you see his strategy throughout Scripture. In Genesis 15:4–6, Satan, using Abraham's wife, Sarah, caused Abraham to doubt whether or not God would be faithful to His promise to make him into a great nation. In the end, Abraham took measures into his own hands and had relations with Sarah's servant, Hagar. Ishmael—and a whole slew of trouble— was born (Gen. 16). And Satan does the same thing with us.

Here's a personal story of Satan's schemes. Lately, God has convicted my husband and me about the amount of sugar we eat. We've felt Him asking us to limit our intake and exhibit some self-control in our eating habits. I wish I could tell you how many times Satan has whispered in my ear: "Amanda, did God really say that you couldn't eat that piece of cake?"

If we aren't willing to be obedient to God in the small areas of our lives, then we will not be obedient when the stakes are high.

(And while I'm being honest, I tend to be an emotional eater, and sugar is my drug of choice.) Of course, the consequence of eating one piece of cake isn't detrimental. But, the principle of obedience still applies.

Ladies, if we aren't willing to be obedient to God in the small areas of our lives, then we will not be obedient when the stakes are high. When Satan comes against us to question God's Word, we must fight him with the power of God's Word. That means, we must *know* God's Word and have it hidden in our hearts and minds (Ps. 119:11; Eph. 6:10–18; Heb. 4:12). Instead of turning to Adam and getting the real scoop on what God said about the tree of knowledge, Eve barged forward in her strength and tried to win a word's game with the devil (Gen. 3:2–5). Don't make the same mistake as Eve. If you think you can tangle with the devil and win, then you are dead wrong. If we don't fight Satan with Scripture, then he will eat our spiritual (and maybe even physical) lunch.

 REST STOP: How is Satan using "Did God really say ..." to tempt you to sin?

What actions can you take to shut his mouth? What Bible verses or passages you can memorize so you can fight Satan at a moment's notice?

I want you to notice something else in this chapter. We've already made a passing glance at it, but I want us to really study and look at the consequences of it. After Eve spoke with the serpent, Scripture says, "So she took some of its fruit and ate it; she also gave some to her husband, *who was with her*, and he ate it" (Gen. 3:6 emphasis added*). What?* Did we read that correctly? Adam was with her while she was taking a bite from the delightful fruit? Yep! In that moment, Adam should have stepped up, taken the fruit from her, and reminded her of what God really said. Instead, he stepped back, abdicated his role as the spiritual leader of his family, and allowed Eve—and then himself—to plow headlong into sin. The results of that one action were devastating. Genesis 3:7 says that in an instant, "the eyes of both of them were opened, and they knew they were naked." For the first time, the man and the woman—the image-bearers of God—felt shame.

This passage of Scripture takes the breath out of me. What are your thoughts and feelings when you read Genesis 3:6–7?

Thinking back on Adam's role as the spiritual leader of his family, do you see the importance of his role as leader and protector? Explain your answer.

NOT-SO-DESIGNER FIG LEAVES
AND THE BLAME GAME

Before we study the judgments God placed on the serpent, Eve, and then Adam, don't miss the lesson found at the end of Genesis 3:7. Scripture says that Adam and Eve tried to cover up their nakedness (shame) with fig leaves. I've never worn underwear made from leaves, but I'm sure they are not very comfortable. Not only that, but they don't last. When my husband gets me flowers, they are beautiful for a couple of days, and then they begin to whither. So, not only are the first man and woman covered in shame, but they are covered in rotten leaves. Before we turn our nose up to them, let me point out that we do the same thing. We sin. We get caught. Then, we try to cover it up.

King David is familiar with this scenario. Read 1 Samuel 11.

Where was David supposed to be (1 Sam. 11:1)?

What was the progression of David's sinful choices?

If we don't immediately come to God, fall on our faces before Him, confess our sin to Him, and then ask for His forgiveness, our life will take the same path as David's. God is abounding in mercy and His forgiveness is unending, but we must come to Him (1 John 1:9).

Before casting Adam and Eve out of the garden, God killed an animal (made atonement for their sin), and then clothed them (Gen. 3:21). You see, withering, rotting fig leaves couldn't cover up their sin, just as our excuses and feeble attempts of self-denial and humiliation can't cover up our sin. Only the blood of an animal—and later the blood of a perfect Lamb, Jesus—can take away our sin and restore our relationship with God (Heb. 9:22).

REST STOP: Are you trying to cover up sin in your life? If so, what is stopping you from coming to God's throne of grace and asking for His forgiveness and deliverance? Look at Hebrews 4:14–16. He will delight to bring you freedom!

The next part of the chapter, Genesis 3:8–13, reads like a good, but tragic, story. There is suspense, deceit, and fighting among the main characters. Adam is in the garden—wearing his not-so-designer fig leaf loincloth—and he hears God walking through the garden. Swish swash, swish swash—He's getting closer—*swish swash*. All of a sudden, he hears God's voice. "Adam, where are you?" Because Adam is the spiritual leader and head of his family, God goes straight to him. However, Adam is playing a game of hide and seek (sin seems to bring that out in us).

Lest you think God physically lost Adam during the time he ate of the fruit until now, let me clarify what God was really asking. God is questioning Adam like a father would question a child. If you have children, then you've probably asked this question a time or two. You sense they have pulled away from you, so you sit them down and have a family meeting. In seeking to get to their heart, you ask, "Where are you? What happened to my sweet, loving child?" Just like you want them to confess when or how they went wrong, God is asking the same of Adam. God knew Adam had sinned, and He knew reconciliation would not happen unless Adam first admitted and owned up to his sin.

I want to point out that Adam had a choice, to tell the truth or skirt around the issue. He chose the latter. Adam confessed he was naked, but he never confessed his sin. To get His answer, God had to specifically ask him if he had eaten of the tree of knowledge. Look back at Genesis 3:12 to see Adam's response. Instead of admitting that he sinned, Adam played the blame game. "That woman you gave me did it! It's all her fault!" In her defense, Eve said, "It wasn't me! It was the serpent who *made* me do it!" And, all the while, Satan is smiling—for now.

At the time of this writing, I have a three-year-old and a two-year-old. For two years, I've looked forward to the day when they would play together and didn't need me to constantly entertain them. Well, that day has come. It's sweet to watch them interact and laugh with each other, and their conversations melt my heart. However, it doesn't take long before I hear one of them scream out in frustration. As soon as I walk in the room, the blame game begins. "Mommy, Hannah is provoking me to anger!" Said by my three-year-old. "But Mommy, KK took my doll!" Said by my two-year-old. "But, Hannah was done with it! No, I wasn't!" Unless I call a time out, these blasts of accusations would go on forever. I didn't teach them to blame each other. It comes with the territory. When confronted with our own sin, we are tempted to shift blame off of us and onto another.

Does this sound familiar? Are you tempted to blame your husband, coworker, friends, or your children for your sin? Why is it so hard to admit when we have done something wrong?

The blame game didn't work for Adam and Eve, and it definitely won't work for us. When we sin, God is looking to us to come clean. Only then can He give us healing, forgiveness, and restore us back into a relationship with Him.

THE CURSE AND ROLE CONFUSION

We have finally come to the focal point of our week. Let's look at the final section of Genesis 3. Read Genesis 3:14–19.

What are your initial thoughts on these verses?

The Serpent

In Genesis 3:14–15, God curses the serpent—the animal that Satan possessed. To be clear, "God's condemnation is not directed against the reptile, per se, but the adversary that it represents."[14] What did the curse actually involve?

There are three judgments God pronounced on the serpent. First, he would crawl on his belly. Some scholars believe that snakes used to walk around on legs. Of course, no one knows that for sure, but Scripture does make a pretty good case. The second part was that he would eat dust, which would naturally come from his belly crawl. The last pronouncement is the most significant. Genesis 3:15 says, "I will put hostility between you and the woman, and between your seed and her seed. He will strike your head, and you will strike his heel." This verse is called the *protevangelium*. This is a very long word, but look at it closely.

What word do you see in *protevangelium*?

Protevangelium is a Latin word meaning "the first preaching of [the] gospel."[15] Right here, in the midst of their sin and shame, God gave Adam and Eve hope. He foreshadowed the coming of Jesus and promised that Satan would ultimately be defeated. Satan had tempted them and succeeded, but one day he would be destroyed.

I don't know about you, but that puts a little jump in my step. This life is so difficult—and there are days when we seem to lose more spiritual battles than we would like to admit—but God hasn't forgotten us. Over two thousand years ago, God fulfilled His promise when He sent Jesus to die on a cruel, rugged cross. Our Savior took our sin and shame, died, lay in a grave for three days, and then rose again. Ladies, we can experience victory over our sin—including sin in our present life. We no longer have to be held captive by the schemes of the Enemy. God has won. And one day Satan will be bound up and thrown into hell (Rev. 20:10). Can I please get a Hallelujah?!

REST STOP: What sin are you carrying? Would you be willing to cast it at the foot of the cross and allow God—through the blood of Jesus—to give you victory? What steps do you need to take to make that a reality in your life?

The Woman

God then turned His attention toward Eve. He told her, "I will intensify your labor pains; you will bear children in anguish. Your desire will be for your husband, yet he will rule over you" (Gen. 3:16).

There are two judgments God pronounced on Eve. The first was in regards to childbirth. As we saw last week, God commanded the couple to "be fruitful, multiply, [and] fill the earth" (Gen. 1:28). God is the giver of life, so bearing children has always been part of His plan. But now, instead of a divine epidural, women would experience pain during childbirth—thank you, Eve. (As amazing as childbirth is, I could have done without the labor pains.)

The second judgment involved the relationship between Adam and Eve. Before they sinned, Adam and Eve lived in perfect harmony with God and each other. The man was the protector, provider, and spiritual leader of his family, while the woman was his helper. Then one day Adam decided to not stand up as the spiritual leader, and everything changed. Instead of harmony, God stated, "Your desire will be for your husband, yet he will rule over you."

Genesis 3:16 has entire books written about it, so we will only scratch the surface in this section. However, I think we can come to a good understanding of what God told the woman. Just so you know, for decades scholars have debated questions such as, Does this verse signify a distortion of gender roles or the introduction of gender roles? Does God give Adam permission to beat his wife? What does this judgment really mean?

What do you think about the above questions? Before I explain them, what do you think God's judgment on the woman means?

Let's look at the first part of the sentence: "Your desire will be for your husband" (Gen. 3:16a). The Hebrew word for "desire" is the word *teshuqah* meaning "a longing, desire, a very strong emotion or feeling to have or do something." It comes from the Hebrew word *shûwq* (pronounced shook) meaning "to run after or over."[16]

To help us better understand this phrase, read Genesis 4:7.

What was after Cain? What was he to do about it?

God told Eve that she would still desire to be with her husband, but that desire would be tainted by sin. Sin would now cause the woman to not only physically desire her husband but also desire to dominate and rule over him.[17] God's original design was for men and women to find joy and fulfillment in the responsibilities given to them in Genesis 2, but sin destroyed that contentment. Now, they would struggle for who was in charge.

Ladies, we all feel the effects of this judgment and struggle with our role as helper. I was thirty-one years old when I married, which means I spent thirteen years living as a single woman. You can imagine the adjustment—and, at times, the frustration—of living with a man. My husband is a great

> ℘ ℘
>
> *God's original design was for men and women to find joy and fulfillment in the responsibilities given to them in Genesis 2, but sin destroyed that contentment. Now, they would struggle for who was in charge.*
>
> ℘ ℘

leader, but he moves a little slower than I do—on everything. He is calculated in almost every decision he makes, and he is careful to weigh all the options before he jumps in. I am totally opposite of that. I am rational, but I like to make quick decisions and get on with life. If you come to me for counsel, I struggle to resist the urge to give you a list of solutions and send you on your way. So you can imagine the learning curve I had when I said, "I do." After five years of marriage, I have learned how to step back and let Chris lead. But, it comes with the overwhelming temptation to take back control.

If you are married, how has the desire to rule over your husband played out in your marriage? If you aren't married, do you feel the temptation to dominate or control dating relationships?

The second part of the sentence says, "yet he will rule over you" (Gen. 3:16b). The Hebrew word used for "rule" normally "refers to ruling by greater power or force or strength."[18] It is not a word that means a rule among equals, but it is a ruling of a stronger person over a weaker person. Before you accuse the Bible of condoning spousal abuse, let's look at its context. (And, if you are being physically, emotionally, or sexually abused by your husband, please get help. Nowhere in Scripture do you see God encouraging or condoning wife abuse. It is a crime, and it should be punished.) God just told Eve that she would desire to rule over her husband, instead of lovingly submitting under Adam's authority and being his helpmate. In response, he would be tempted to dominate her (rule with force), instead of being a servant leader who provided for and protected his family.

Do you see the distortion? The responsibilities God created were perfect and were intended to bring harmony to the marriage relationship. And now, with sin in the equation, that harmony was disrupted. Marriage is often defined by a power struggle between two people who are supposed to love each other. Ladies, this was not God's design or initial plan. Obviously, because He is an all-knowing God, He knew sin would enter the world. Though, for a moment, however long it took between Genesis 2 and 3 to occur, God allowed Adam and Eve to experience what marriage could be like when God was the One in control of their marriage.

 REST STOP: What about you? Do you believe Genesis 3 invented or distorted the original roles of men and women in marriage?

How does God want you to respond? Are you and your husband in a battle for who is in control? What would life be like if you laid down your "weapons" and asked your husband how you can help him?

I realize these questions can be tough to answer. You may be in a marriage where fighting is the norm. Some of you may be in a marriage where there isn't visible fighting, but you realize your husband has become withdrawn or passive-aggressive. I have a challenge for you. Take a week and step back from the reigns. Let your husband lead, and ask how you can help and encourage him. (You may have to pick up his jaw off the floor, but don't let that detour you. Let him know you are serious and sincere.) See what God can do in your marriage when you make an attempt to do marriage according to His design. You will find God's blessings abound—I promise!

The Man

The last one to receive judgment was Adam.

Read Genesis 3:17–19. What were the judgments placed on Adam?

In Genesis 3:17–19, God told Adam that the ground would be cursed and would produce thorns and briars. God would still allow plants to grow, which gave Adam the means to work and provide for his family, but it wouldn't be easy. In Genesis 2:15, work was to be a blessing and joy for him. Man was supposed to find his fulfillment in the work God gave him. Even now, God, in His grace and compassion, allows man to sometimes enjoy his work. However, there is a difference. Work is now painful, sweaty, difficult, and a necessity for survival.

In Genesis 3, Satan began with a simple lie, and Eve bought it, hook, line, and sinker. Satan also told her that she wouldn't die from eating the fruit. And, initially, he was correct. Adam and Eve didn't physically die, but their eyes were opened. They had a knowledge they couldn't handle. They could now distinguish between good and evil.

But other aspects of their lives were also affected. Their relationship with God wasn't as intimate as it was before sin entered the world. He couldn't walk with them as He did before the fall. Therefore, God erected a spiritual and physical barrier between Him and sinful man (Gen. 3:23–24). Their relationship with each other was distorted and challenged. Instead of living in harmony, they would spend their days fighting for control. And lastly, man's relationship with the ground was affected. Instead of continual life, the ground would produce thorns and, after they died, would eventually receive them back as dust.

WE'VE MADE A MESS OF THINGS

With the pronouncement of judgment, you would think Adam and Eve would alter their course and teach their children how to live in unity with each other. However, sin is a cruel taskmaster. With every passing generation, man and woman have grown further and further away from God's original design. Not convinced? Let me give you a little history lesson on just how far we've traveled. It may get a little tedious, but hang in there with me.

The 1950s were the golden years of America. That era inspired TV shows like *Leave It to Beaver, The Andy Griffith Show*, and *Lassie*. Mothers were depicted as caring women who had supper and a kiss ready and waiting for their husband when he came home from work. The dad was the strong leader of the family and the primary breadwinner. However, a fierce attack on manhood and womanhood was beginning.

In 1949, Simone de Beauvoir's published her book *The Second Sex*. Simone de Beauvoir was a French scholar, whose work would later inspire Betty Friedan—the "mother" of the Feminist Movement. In *The Second Sex*, de Beauvoir said that the male-dominated society called and treated women as the "Other"—meaning women had no real identity or existence apart from their relationship to a man. She was frustrated because she felt like women were treated as subjects of men and had no real role apart from being a wife, a mother, and cleaning the house. Later on, she would be one of the first to emphatically say, "One is not born, but rather becomes, a woman."[19]

Let's fast-forward about fifteen years. Simone de Beauvoir's work didn't gain a lot of traction with the masses, but it started a conversation. We now move to the era of the Hippie and Free Love Movement. People's minds are more open to new ideas, and challenging the status quo is considered a good thing.

In 1963, Betty Friedan published her infamous book *The Feminine Mystique*. Her book was the rallying cry behind the

Feminist Movement of the 1960–1970s. (You may not know the book, but I'm sure you've heard of the movement it inspired.) It was during this portion of American history when women began to have the courage to question their place in society. Friedan's work hit a nerve with these women seeking freedom, because she dared to ask the same question they were asking, "Is this all?"[20]

You may be thinking, "That's a lot of information, but what does it have to do with me? I'm no feminist." That might be true. But, you may be more of a feminist than you realize; I certainly was. You may never have heard of Simone de Beauvoir or Betty Friedan, but you are living the effects of their influence. Working women are not the exception but the norm. I no longer ask a high school senior if she is going to college because I assume she is. Mothers now have a choice—to work inside or outside the home. And most often, they choose outside the home. And the most disturbing effect: de Beauvoir's claim that womanhood and femininity are not given at birth but something that a woman becomes if she so chooses is no longer questioned. It's actually celebrated.

To be fair, the Feminist Movement has also brought about some positive effects. A woman is a respected and a valuable asset to organizations and companies. A woman has a voice and can state that voice without being dismissed. And, most importantly, a woman is encouraged to pursue and use an educational degree. (This was definitely a blessing to me.) But we can't ignore what the Feminist Movement cost us—

We will come to discover that Jesus' death, burial, and resurrection didn't reverse the gender roles God established, but it redeemed them.

the contentment of resting and finding fulfillment in our God-ordained and designed roles.

What did you learn from our history lesson? What positive ways have you been affected by the Feminist Movement? What are some of the negative effects? Explain.

Several years ago, I heard someone say, "sin will take you farther than you want to go, keep you longer than you want to stay, and cost you more than you want to pay." I think we can agree with this statement. What started as one simple bite led to corruption and death.

But God had a plan; He always does. That plan came in the form of a baby named Jesus. He lived the sinless life we couldn't live and then paid the price for sin that we could never pay. We will come to discover that Jesus' death, burial, and resurrection didn't reverse the gender roles God established, but it redeemed them. In fact, that is the topic of next week's study.

Ladies, I'm so glad you are still with me. You are doing great! Now, go grab yourself a cup of coffee, or the comfort drink of your choice. See you next week.

GETTING BACK ON TRACK:
GOD'S DESIGN FOR MARRIAGE

Welcome back! I feared I would lose you last week, so hear me take a huge sigh of relief. I never want you to feel condemned. Instead, know I am praying for you as you continue to struggle and work through your own thoughts and emotions regarding womanhood. I am right there with you. Just because I've written a Bible study on biblical womanhood doesn't mean that I don't struggle from time to time. Learning to die to the flesh and become obedient to God's Word is difficult—it's like trying to fit into your skinny jeans after you've gorged on chocolate cake. Not easy, and at times, not very pretty. But, by God's grace working in us, we can be the women He created us to be. Let's do this together!

UNDERSTANDING THE CONTEXT

This week we will turn our attention to marriage. (If you aren't married, please don't skip this week. You will find nuggets of truth in here to help as you wait for God's best.) We are also moving from the Old Testament to the New Testament, looking specifically at the marriage passages found in Ephesians and Colossians.

Read Ephesians 5–6:1–9 and Colossians 3. Write down what Paul discusses in these chapters.
Ephesians 5–6:1–9:

Colossians 3:

Did you find some common themes? Typically, when a pastor teaches on marriage, he immediately jumps to Ephesians 5:22–33 or Colossians 3:18–19. Rarely, if ever, do you see these passages in their context. So, along with what you wrote, I want you to see exactly what surrounds Paul's teaching on marriage.

At the time of his writing, Paul was imprisoned in Rome for his faith in Jesus and his relentless preaching of the gospel. (In my opinion, prison isn't the best writing venue, but at least it made Paul stop long enough to put pen to paper.) Paul wrote Ephesians and Colossians about the same time, which is roughly AD 60.[21] If you took time to read both books in their entirety, which I strongly recommend, then you will discover these books are similar in format and content. They both discuss:

- Putting off the old self and putting on the new self (Eph. 4:22–24; Col. 3:9–10)
- The mystery of the gospel—Christ in you (Eph. 3:1–6; Col. 1:24–27)
- Commands for Christian living (Eph. 5:1–5; Col. 3:5–9)
- Roles of men and women in marriage (Eph. 5:22–33; Col. 3:18–19)
- Relationship between father and child (Eph. 6:1–4; Col. 3:20–21)
- Relationship between masters and slaves (Eph. 6:5–9; Col. 3:22–4:1)

You can see the roles of men and women are just one theme among many. The overarching purpose of these books is to show Christians that Jesus—through the Holy Spirit living and working in them—should be the One in control of every aspect of their lives.

In reading Scripture, make sure you don't isolate an individual passage from the rest of the book. (This is a good principle for all Bible study.) In both Ephesians and Colossians, the marriage passage comes right after Paul tells the church how a Christian should act and relate in the world. You can almost hear Paul setting us up for something important. He tells us, "As a Christian, you should treat all people with respect, love, and show thanksgiving for them in your life." (This is Amanda's loosely translated version.) He goes on to describe how each relationship (husband/wife, parents/children, and masters/slaves—employer/employee) are to relate to each other. Remember, in these passages, Paul is speaking to Christians.

Another aspect of the context involves the time period in which Ephesians and Colossians were written. In Paul's day, women were not respected nor seen as having equal value with men. (Somehow they missed God's teaching on equality in Genesis 1.) Men were allowed to be harsh with their wives and even divorce them without a cause. Therefore, women were often left without money and protection, resulting in being seen as an outcast in society. This doesn't sound like a very good time period to live.

Paul, raised and educated as a Pharisee, was taught and had modeled to him this mistreatment of women. Yet, upon meeting Christ (Acts 9), Paul was transformed into a new creation (2 Cor. 5:17). What an incredible display of God's transforming power and restoration! Therefore, when Paul teaches about relationships—especially marriage—he gives instructions to *both* men and women.

Paul's approach to marriage instruction was a foreign idea in the ancient culture. Since men could treat their wives however they chose, instructions to love their wives went against everything Paul and the rest of the men were taught. Not only were husbands to love their wives, but they were to treat their wives with respect and cherish them as they would their own bodies.[22] (You can almost hear the men exclaim, "Do what?! You want me to love *and* cherish my wife? Isn't she my property?") Therefore, as we study these passages, have an open mind and ask God to show you what He wants to teach you. Don't get stuck on the whole idea of submission that you miss the greater truth and reality of these passages. I think God is going to blow your spiritual socks off and leave you in awe of Him. Now, let's dig into Ephesians 5:22–33.

SUBMISSION: IT ISN'T A FOUR-LETTER WORD

Both in Ephesians 5:22–24 and Colossians 3:18, Paul addresses the women first. So, that is where we will begin.

Read those verses, and then respond. What is your initial reaction to God's command for a wife to submit to her husband?

I think I know what some of you are thinking—I've thought it myself. "What in the world does Paul mean by *submit*? If you think I'm going to lie down and let a man walk all over me, then you're dead wrong!" You will be happy to know that being submissive to your husband doesn't mean that you are to be a doormat. However, it *does* mean you are commanded to be respectful and come under your husband's leadership and authority as the head of your family. But, I am getting ahead of myself.

Submission Defined in Marriage

First, let's look at the biblical definition of submission. Remember how I told you that we often miss the full meaning of a passage because the Bible was originally written in another language? Because of our limited English vocabulary, we have come to another one of those misunderstood words: "submit."

The New Testament was written in Greek, and then translated into other languages. In both passages, the Greek verb used for "submit" is the word *hupotassō*. In its simplest definition, *hupotassō* means to "place or arrange under, to submit one's control, to yield to one's admonition or advice."[23]

Do you see a common theme in this definition?

So what is true, biblical submission? *Hupotassō* does not mean forced submission—abuse—or give the one in authority the right to humiliate the one in submission.[24] Instead, *hupotassō* is best understood as a military term used to describe a private who *voluntarily* comes under the authority of his superior officer.[25] (In case you missed it, the answer to the above question is biblical submission is a voluntary decision, not as a result of force.)

I've never served in the military, so I don't claim to understand the life of a soldier. But I have friends who have served, and I've seen movies that try to capture what they go through day in and day out. At the time of this writing, the movie *American Sniper* is making waves in the theatres. It details the life of Navy SEAL Chris Kyle, the best sniper in American military history. (For the record, I normally don't go to movies with a lot of violence in them. But, it was amazing to see the heroism of a man like Chris.) One of my favorite scenes was when Chris left his post as sniper and joined the enlisted guys as they went door to door looking for bad guys. Chris, being a chief petty officer, didn't have to get down into the nitty-gritty of battle, and his comrade tried to convince him to remain up on the roof. But Chris recognized that he, being both an officer and a soldier, had a duty to serve his men. His men also had the responsibility to submit under his leadership. They needed each other, and they had to work together in order to accomplish their mission.

Ladies, this story, in a way, depicts the marriage relationship. Both the husband and the wife are given certain commands, but they need each other to make it work. A wife must choose to give up her desire to lead and come under her husband's authority. And, a husband must control his desire to rule over his wife and respond to her with love and servant leadership. (We will get to that later.)

Secondly, let's look at whom exactly a woman is to submit under.

Read Ephesians 5:22. Who must a wife submit under?

A woman is not responsible to submit to every man in every situation. She is to submit to her own husband. That means, unless your husband is my boss or pastor, I don't have to submit to him. (Even submission to your employer and/or pastor is different from submission to your husband.) We are asked to respect all men in the same way that God asks us to respect all people, but we don't have to submit to them. So please don't buy into the lie that the Bible teaches that all women are under the authority of all men. That just isn't the case.

The Appeal of Submission

As to the Lord

Paul said that wives are to submit to their husbands "as to the Lord" (Eph. 5:22b). First, let me explain what this phrase does not mean. It *does not* mean a woman is to submit to her husband in the same way she would submit to Christ. If your husband asks you to do something immoral or illegal, then don't do it. Your first responsibility is to obey the commands of God.

However, this phrase *does* mean that a wife must submit to her husband even when she does not like or agree with his choices. For example, your husband comes in and announces that he has decided to buy a dog to protect the family and the house from intruders. He also thinks it would be a good pet to help your children learn responsibility. You do not like dogs nor do you want the responsibility of having to train a dog. (Um ... that would be me.) After conversing with your husband and giving him your opinion and reasoning for not wanting a dog, he decides that a dog is what is best for the family. At that point, you have a decision to make. Will you submit under his leadership and what he thinks is best for the family? Or will you put your foot down and get nasty? (At some point, we've all done this.)

Have you ever had a situation like this come up in your marriage? If so, explain. What was the outcome?

I realize the above example is trivial, but it holds a great truth. We are so tempted to fight our husbands over decisions that are nonissues and refuse to allow them to lead our family. I am not saying that women do not have a right to be heard in the marriage relationship—we do. However, when our husbands make a decision, and it doesn't go against God's Word, then we must show them the respect they deserve. This is a hard truth, but I'm going to say it anyway: It is preposterous for a woman to boast in her love and submission to God's authority, yet she demonstrates, by her attitude and actions, a blatant disregard for her husband's leadership and authority in their marriage.

Comparing Two "Heads"

Read Ephesians 5:23–24. In this passage, what is being compared?

We have finally reached the purpose behind a wife's submission. If marriage is a picture of Christ and His church—and it is—as a wife submits to her husband, she is representing and modeling to a spiritually lost person how they are to come to God. She is also demonstrating how the church, Christ's bride, should respond to Him with submission.

ഇ⊃ ⊂ഓ

It is preposterous for a woman to boast in her love and submission to God's authority, yet she demonstrates by her attitude and actions a blatant disregard for her husband's leadership and authority in their marriage.

ഇ⊃ ⊂ഓ

Though Jesus is the perfect Bridegroom and my husband is not, when I practice submitting to Christ, then I can more easily submit to my husband. Ladies, we have an opportunity to hold up our marriage as a picture of the gospel. (What an exciting thought!) Do you want your life to proclaim the gospel of Jesus? Then accept the leadership of your husband as the head of your family.

So, how are you doing? In your spiritual life, are you struggling to submit to Jesus? In your marriage, are you struggling (or refusing) to submit to your husband?

REST STOP: Ask God to help you continue to love, respect, and submit, first to Him and then to your husband's leadership. Wherever you are in your marriage, I want you to write out a prayer expressing your heart in this matter. Know I am also praying for you.

Common Questions about Submission

Nearly every time I teach on submission, there are a number of common objections and questions women ask me. Many times, these questions are nonbiblical assumptions about the command to submit. You may be thinking these as well. My prayer is that this list helps clear up any confusion on what the Bible does and does not teach about a wife's role.

I have a friend whose husband is physically and emotionally abusive to her. What should she do?

Please hear me loud and clear: if you are in an abusive relationship, you need to find a safe place. Know that God does not condone abuse, and it breaks His heart to see His child hurting. As we have studied, the command for a wife to submit to her husband does not mean that her husband has permission to hurt her. I'm not saying that you have to divorce him, but your safety and the safety of your children should be your first priority. After you are safe, then you, with a good Christian counselor by your side, can decide what to do.

Am I supposed to submit to my husband if he asks me to do something illegal or immoral?

And once again, I give a resounding *no*! A woman's first responsibility is to be obedient to God and His Word. If your husband asks you to do something illegal, then you must respectfully refuse to do it. (It may also be necessary to get the law enforcement involved.)

The same is true for immoral activity. If your husband (or boyfriend for those who aren't married) asks you to engage in any immoral activity, then you must also refuse. I've had women tell me their husband wants them to look at pornography with them to help put a spark back in their relationship. Ladies, please don't go there. It will further damage you and your marriage.

Am I supposed to submit to my husband if he is not a Christian?

Yes! If your husband is not a Christian, then it is your responsibility to pray for him and then live out a godly life in front of him. It will not be easy. But, you can do more damage to your marriage and your testimony as a Christian if you don't submit to him.

In 1 Corinthians 7:12–16, Paul makes the statement that a husband could become a follower of Christ because of the witness of his wife. I have a friend who became a Christian after she was married. Both of them were wild, and then she met Jesus. After years of watching his wife's behavior change toward him, their children, and others, he eventually became a Christian. What a powerful testimony of how God can use your example to change your husband's life!

If you aren't married, then you are in a great position. In understanding the roles of men and women in marriage, I pray you have seen the importance of marrying a godly man. Marriage is difficult. It is even more difficult when you marry a man who does not share your love for Jesus. Even if he is cute, funny, and has a great personality, if he doesn't love Jesus, then *do not date him*! You will marry who you date.

Am I supposed to submit to my husband when he doesn't love me as Christ loves the church?

Yes! This is a common objection that women give for not wanting to submit to their husbands. I've actually had women tell me, "I will submit to my husband when he begins to love me like Christ loves the church!" (Maybe you've even said or thought those words.) There is just one little problem: Ephesians 5:22–24 does not give an escape clause. God doesn't say, "Wives submit to your husband as long as he loves you like Christ loves the church." Instead, God gives us a direct command. Your obedience to God's commands is not based on your husband's obedience to God's commands. We all are called to obey, regardless of the other's obedience, or lack thereof.

Do any of these objections resonate in your spirit? If so, which one?

Do you have your own excuse for not submitting to your husband? Describe your struggle here.

Ladies, I pray you have seen that submission is more than just something to push back against. My prayer is God allows you to see His glorious design of marriage and the blessing of being obedient to the roles He has given. We've dealt with women's roles; now let's switch our attention to the role of men. I have some exciting things to show you.

ALL YOU NEED IS LOVE

A Woman's Greatest Need

God uniquely fashioned man and woman and gave us differing needs.

When you are in a serious relationship, or even desiring a relationship, what is it that you most want from the guy?

My guess is that most of you just answered, "I want to be and feel loved!" I still remember the day my husband expressed to me the fullness of his love. This declaration was different from his typical affirmation of love, so it got my attention. We were engaged, talking and making plans for our future, and then it happened. He looked at me—his eyes full of love and joy—and exclaimed, "Amanda, you are so beautiful, and I can't wait to begin our life together. I want you to know that I love you, *you!*" He loved *me*—and only me. He loved me despite my flaws, my accomplishments, my abilities, and even with my sin. *Wow!*

Describe a time when you first heard the words, "I love you."

How did it make you feel?

Ladies, God, in His wisdom, made me and you with a desire to be loved. With this in mind, I want us to look at Ephesians 5:25–31 and explore what this passage commands husbands to do.

What metaphors does God use to describe the kind of love a husband should have toward his wife?

Do you think this comes easy for him? Why?

Exploring the Command

There are three kinds of love mentioned in this passage. English has only one word for love. However, the Greek language has three different words: *agape* (Godlike love), *phileo* (brotherly/friendship love) and *eros* (passionate/sexual love). I can say, "I love coffee! And I love my husband for bringing me a cup!" Obviously, you know I'm not speaking of the same type or intensity of love. In Ephesians 5:25–31, God specifically gives men three ways or kinds of love to show his wife.

Godlike Love

"Husbands, love your wives, just as Christ loved the church and gave Himself for her" (Eph. 5:25). In this verse, Paul uses the Greek word *agapoō*. This word for love is a self-sacrificing love and a love that is Godlike. Only God, through the power of the Holy Spirit, can produce *agape* love within an individual.[26] Men (and women for that matter) don't naturally have *agape* love flowing through them.

You know more about *agape* love than you realize. First Corinthians 13 defines it in detail. "Love is patient, love is kind. Love does not envy, is not boastful, is not conceited, does not act improperly, is not selfish, is not provoked, and does not keep a record of wrongs. Love finds no joy in unrighteousness but rejoices in the truth. It bears all things, believes all things, hopes all things, endures all things. Love never ends" (1 Cor. 13:4–8). What a list!

REST STOP: Does 1 Corinthians 13:4–8 define your love for others? If not, what are some effective, practical changes you can make?

God's command to the husband is powerful and, by God's grace, humanly possible. Just as Jesus gave up His life for His bride, the church, husbands are to have such a self-sacrificing love for their wife that they would be willing to die for her. This means that the only way a man can and will love his wife with *agape* love is through a relationship with Christ. In a world where love is based on feelings and actions instead of a commitment, this type of self-sacrificing love is unique.

Sanctifying Love

Ephesians 5:26 says Jesus' love toward His church is designed, "to make her holy, cleansing her with the washing of water by the word." This is a sanctifying love. The word "sanctify" means to be set apart, especially for holy use. Though Ephesians 5:26 is specifically focused on Christ sanctifying His bride, the church, Paul also makes the comparison that a husband should love his wife with a sanctifying love. Don't be confused. This passage doesn't teach that your salvation is dependent upon your husband. But it does mean a husband is to have a love for his wife that is set apart from any other love in his life. God even gives husbands a tangible

But it does mean a husband is to have a love for his wife that is set apart from any other love in his life. God even gives husbands a tangible way to sanctify his wife—by washing his wife with God's Word. Simply put, he is to speak Scripture over her life.

way to sanctify his wife—by washing his wife with God's Word. Simply put, he is to speak Scripture over her life.

When she is struggling, he is to take her to God's Word for encouragement and strength. When there is a decision to make, a husband should make it after he has sought God's counsel. I love how one commentator described it: "If a husband loves his wife as Christ loved the church, his love and care will have a sanctifying influence on the wife, who will experience personal benefit and progress as a result. The wife will never be perfect, but *she becomes more than she would* if the husband does not love her as Christ loved the church" (emphasis added).[27]

I am a testimony of the sanctifying love of a great husband. When I met my husband, I had just started my doctoral work. We married six months later. Seven months later, we were expecting our first daughter. I was barely two years into doctoral work, and I was going to be a mother. Makaylan was born, and five months later, we were pregnant again. There is no reason, except for God's strength and my husband's constant love and encouragement, that I should have finished my program. But, I did. Chris's love and support turned me into a better, more productive wife, mother, and student.

What about you? If you are married, how has your husband's love made you a better woman? If you aren't married, do you need to change the type of guys you date in order to have this type of love in your marriage?

Nurturing Love

In Ephesians 5:28–31, Paul continues the marriage metaphor by returning to the husband-wife relationship. He says that a husband is to love and care for, or nurture, his wife as he does his own body. Our natural desire is to take care of ourselves first. We get hungry, so we feed our bodies. When we get thirsty, we get something to drink. When we exercise, we get stronger and feel better about ourselves. Therefore, the command to care for and nurture invalidates any misunderstanding that God gives men permission to abuse or hurt their wives. In Colossians 3:19, Paul specifically mentions abuse when he instructs husbands to not be harsh with their wives.

I also want to point out that God commands men to do something that is not naturally characteristic of men. Women are known as nurturers. When my girls hurt themselves, they come running to mommy. They love their daddy, but mommy is the one who holds them close, lets them cry, and kisses their boo-boos. However, in the marriage relationship, God commands husbands to step outside of what is natural for them in order to show their wife a tender, compassionate, Godlike love.

In Ephesians 5:31, Paul appeals to Genesis 2:24. Paul reminds the husband that he has a responsibility to leave his family of origin and be completely united ("glued together, cement, fasten firmly") with his wife. A wife should be the most important person in a man's life.[28] As a result of this marriage union, the husband and wife become "one flesh." Therefore, when a husband loves his wife, he actually loves his own body.

REST STOP: What type of love are you in most need of right now? (Godlike, sanctifying, or nurturing) What did God teach you as you studied the loves of Ephesians 5?

The Cost of Love

The husband's command to love his wife is a greater exhortation and comes with a greater cost than the wife's command to submit.

Look back over our passage. Who does Paul spend more time addressing?

Paul spends more time speaking to the husbands than he does wives. As we have studied earlier in the week, men were permitted to treat their wives any way they chose. A husband didn't have to be gentle or loving toward his wife, and yet she was expected, without question, to submit under his authority. Even for a loving husband, Paul raised the standard. It wasn't just good enough for a husband to be kind to his wife. Instead, God wanted him to love his wife with a Godlike love. So you can see how Paul's teaching on marriage was revolutionary and a total paradigm shift for men of his day—and even men in the twenty-first century.

Do you think men have a tendency to be harsh or tender toward women?

What expectations does our society put on men?

Christian men are to be an example for their unbelieving friends and family of how a man treats a woman. In this passage, God is putting His relationship with an unbelieving world on the shoulders of men. He says, "Do you want to know how much I love the church? Look at how a man loves his wife." Ladies, I've said it before, and I will say it again: the gospel of Christ is on display in marriage. So often we want our men to love us and care for us without encouraging and responding to them in a Christlike manner. We want flowers, cards, romantic dinners, and mushy words, but we don't encourage or respond to him when he begins to lead. Yes, God has given women the need to be and feel loved, but we must also appropriately respond to that love instead of holding a grudge for the ways and moments he has not shown love. The burden to love is of great cost to men, and women need to recognize that cost and submit under his leadership.

&)(&

So often we want our men to love us and care for us without encouraging and responding to them in a Christlike manner. We want flowers, cards, romantic dinners, and mushy words, but we don't encourage or respond to him when he begins to lead.

&)(&

THE MYSTERY OF MARRIAGE

Hang in there, sister! We are almost finished. We have finally come to the focal point of the chapter, and it's about to get even better.

What does Paul say in Ephesians 5:32?

What do you think he means?

In Ephesians 5:32, Paul says the marriage relationship is a profound mystery because it represents the relationship between Christ and the church. Despite popular opinion and what we see in movies, marriage is more than just two people falling in love and getting married. Ladies, there is a greater spiritual reality going on when two people decide to join their lives together. Starting with the first marriage ceremony in the Garden of Eden until now, the purpose of marriage is to be a picture of the gospel message. Therefore, marriage is crucial to the glory of God.

However, marriage is being attacked from all sides. There are laws being passed to redefine the marriage relationship. The Supreme Court has decided that marriage can be between two people, regardless of their gender. Marriage, as the union between one man and one woman *for life,* is considered out of date and bigoted. Marriage, little by little, is being destroyed.

What do you see are the results of the reinterpretation of marriage?

Within the church, do you think the marriage relationship is better, worse, or the same? Explain

You see, when it comes to marriage, God expects more than just the status quo, especially for a Christian. The reason divorce breaks God's heart is because it gives a world a picture of an unfaithful God. The reason abuse breaks God's heart is because it gives the world a picture of a harsh, unloving God. The reason a lack of submission breaks God's heart is because it does not give unbelievers a true picture of how a sinner is to come to God. As Christians, we must stand up for the sanctity of marriage. God desires for your marriage, and my marriage, to be a powerful example of His love to a lost world.

There are four main relationships God uses to compare His relationship with His children. He uses the father/child relationship (Rom. 8:15–16), the friend relationship (John 15:15), the Master/servant relationship (Rom. 1:1), and the husband/wife relationship. However, there is only one relationship that God is willing to place His reputation on—and it is

ଽୠ ଔ

The reason divorce breaks God's heart is because it gives a world a picture of an unfaithful God. The reason abuse breaks God's heart is because it gives the world a picture of a harsh, unloving God. The reason a lack of submission breaks God's heart is because it does not give unbelievers a true picture of how a sinner is to come to God.

ଽୠ ଔ

marriage. Ladies, He gives the world permission to ask, "How much does Jesus love His church? And, more importantly, how should His church respond to Him?" His answer: "Look at marriage. Do you see how that man loves his wife? That is how I love my people. Do you see how that woman submits to her husband's leadership? That is how I want my people to respond to me."

The marriage relationship has far greater implications than just one man and one woman living a "happily ever after" life. Fairy tales are good, but there is just one problem: they aren't real. Don't get me wrong, marriage is fun, exciting, and amazing. But, marriage, including the best of marriages, is challenging. I want more for my marriage than what I read in books and what I see on television. I want a God-ordained, God-sized, and God-glorifying marriage.

 REST STOP: What about you? What type of marriage do you want?

What are you doing to help your marriage be an example of the gospel message?

Some of you may be feeling defeated, guilty, or saddened by your marriage. You've made it through the week, barely, but you are so overwhelmed at the state of your marriage that you aren't sure if it will ever look like what Scripture describes. Know you aren't alone. There are women in your church who are exactly where you are. I encourage you to get with them and begin praying for—not bashing—your husbands. Ask God to work, first in you, and then in him. Look for opportunities to encourage your husband and be the helpmate you were created to be. I've seen God do miracles in people's marriages. He can and will do the same for you. Dear sister, I am praying for you. Believe Him for the impossible (Luke 18:27).

Week 4

THE ROAD MAP FOR DISCIPLESHIP:
THE TITUS 2 WOMAN

As I've mention before, I have two daughters ages three and two. (Yes, my house is crazy, and loud, and e-m-o-t-i-o-n-a-l. And, I love it!) A few weeks ago, my husband and I took our girls out to eat. Normally, we eat out every Sunday with either my parents or a college student, so my girls are accustomed to it. However, we rarely eat out with just the four of us. For whatever reason, the girls were exceptionally obnoxious that night. They were all over the place—on the table, under the table, on the floor, they were everywhere but in their seats. I had no clue what was going on with them, and to be honest with you, I was tempted to deny them as my own. Then it hit me, my youngest daughter wasn't in her high chair. We were sitting at a table that didn't have enough room, so we allowed her to get out of her chair and sit like a "big girl." She hadn't practiced sitting in a big chair at home, so her newfound freedom was overwhelming. She wasn't restrained, so she went wild—and I mean *wild*. Her influence was rubbing off on our three-year-old, who knew perfectly well how to sit still. We hurried through dinner, took them home, and then had a "come to Jesus" meeting about restaurant etiquette. We vowed that we would first practice at home before we let Hannah out of her high chair in a public environment again. Even grown women can be flustered when asked to do something unusual in public (spontaneously sharing their testimony, cooking for a big group, or being the "class mom").

Please tell me you can relate. Have you ever asked your child to do something in public that you hadn't practiced at home? I would love to hear the story.

Have you ever been asked to do something before you had an opportunity to practice?

This week we turn our attention to the roles of women within the church. We have studied in depth the roles of men and women within the family, but now it's time to take what we've learned and apply it to the church. The past three weeks will prove to be invaluable as you use them as the backdrop of women's roles within the church.

THE TITUS 2 WOMAN

Hello, My Name Is …

"Hi, my name is Amanda, and I am called to full-time ministry." That is what I felt like saying as I sat in my theology class, being one of two women in the entire class. Normally, my seminary classes were fun and the guys were great, but this one was a little different. It was a May-term, which meant we crammed a semester's worth of work into one week. Since you can get three credit hours in one week, May-terms are usually filled with commuters or people who live out of town. Therefore, in this particular class, I didn't know many of the guys sitting next to me.

My professor thought it would be fun to go down the role and randomly call out people to answer his questions. He got to the first girl, asked her the question, and then waited for her response. "Um … I don't have an opinion about that" was the answer out of her mouth. That's fine. And on he went down the role. Then it was my turn. "Miss Taylor (I wasn't married yet) I'm sure you don't have an opinion about this, but what do you believe women in the church are called to do?" To his amazement, and mine as well, I heard myself proclaim, "Actually, I do have an opinion about that." And I proceeded to answer the question. That class ended up being one of my favorite classes in seminary.

I am often asked how women can be effective in ministry. For many years the only ministry that seemed open to women was children's ministry. So, what were you to do if you, like me, didn't feel called to work in the church nursery or teach a children's Sunday school class? The church overlooked what I call the Titus 2 model of discipleship. This model is defined in Titus 2:3–5, and it's simply this: older, spiritually mature women mentoring and modeling Christlikeness to younger, spiritually immature women.

Since the early 1990s there has been an awakening to the importance of women's Bible study. Writers such as Beth Moore, Priscilla Shirer, Lisa Harper, and Kay Arthur have produced Bible study material to help women grow deeper in their relationship with God and learn more about God's Word. Yet, there is still a misunderstanding of discipleship among the average woman in the local church. Some women have been Christians for decades and have never taken a younger woman under their care in order to teach her God's Word and model to her what it means to be a Jesus follower. Discipleship is still left to the "experts." Let's see if we can change that.

Am I Qualified?

Read Titus 2:3–4. List the five qualifications that Paul states in this passage.

Older Woman

The first qualification is that a woman must be older. If you are reading this sentence, regardless of your age, then you probably qualify for the job. Once again, we turn to the Greek for our clues on how I can be so certain. The Greek word *presbutidas* does mean "an aged or elderly woman," but one must look at the context of these verses in order to gain a fuller understanding of its actual meaning.[29]

In Titus 2:4, Paul gives the context of who these older women were to teach. They were to teach the "young women." The Greek word *neas* is the word translated "young" in the English text. *Neas* is defined as "belonging to the present moment, new, fresh, not previously there, not long there." Therefore, a Titus 2 mentor relationship doesn't necessarily have to be between two women where one woman is chronologically older than another. As long as woman is older in her walk with Jesus and the other is younger in the faith, then a productive and effective discipleship relationship can be birthed.[30]

Why is this so important to understand? Because many women who are older in the faith and capable of teaching a younger woman in the faith often disqualify themselves from the role of discipleship, and they don't consider themselves old enough to fulfill this command. A woman in her forties who has been a Christian for twenty years can disciple a sixty-year-old new convert. Older, mature college-aged women can disciple high school girls. And high school girls can disciple middle school girls. There are younger girls and women in the faith who are hungry for an older woman in the faith to come alongside them and teach them how to grow in Christlikeness.

 REST STOP: What about you? Do you see yourself as an older woman in the faith?

Would you be willing to begin a discipling relationship with someone? Why or why not?

Reverent in Behavior

ℰℭ

In the Greek language, the word *reverent* means "like people engaged in sacred duties, that which is suitable to holiness, temple-like."[31] This word was characteristic of a priest who went about doing his priestly duties of serving, sacrificing, and helping others meet with God. Some of you may be thinking: "Hold up! What? Amanda, I'm no saint! There is no way

A woman who has allowed God to set her apart as holy will not gossip, become enslaved to wine, or slander another. She realizes that God has called all Christians to live their lives to please Him, and people notice she is different. She dresses differently. She speaks differently. She acts differently.

ℰℭ

I can, or maybe even want, to do that. I want to be relevant to people, and walking around with a holier-than-thou attitude won't work." And you're right. No one likes to be around people who think they are better than them. Ladies, we are all on this faith journey together, and we all need each other to survive. A prideful heart, especially one disguised as godly, has no room in ministry. You struggle, and I struggle. However, God does call us to live differently.

Reverent, godly behavior is the overarching theme of Titus 2:3–5. A woman who has allowed God to set her apart as holy will not gossip, become enslaved to wine, or slander another. She realizes that God has called all Christians to live their lives to please Him, and people notice she is different. She dresses differently. She speaks differently. She acts differently. She lives every single day to bring God glory and honor. Ladies, I realize this is a high, and seemingly impossible, calling we have on our life. Please don't disqualify yourself from the role of a discipler because you are more concerned with doing what you want to do instead of what God wants you to do. The world needs women to stand up and live a life consecrated to God.

Do people respect you and know where you stand on moral issues?

 REST STOP: What do you need to change in your life in order to be a woman worthy of respect?

Don't Gossip/Slander Others

Gossip ... this is probably one of the biggest struggles (sin) women face. We all know what a gossip is, and we have all been guilty of it at some point in our lives—maybe even today.

How would you define someone who is a gossip?

Not pretty, huh? The most frustrating thing about a gossip is she looks for faults in another and then spreads that information to others. They bring division and dissension to any group they attend. I don't really like to be around a gossip. In the back of my mind I wonder if she talks about me when I'm not around.

We, as women, enjoy talking. The more we talk, the more vulnerable we are of turning into a gossip. We must guard ourselves against disrespecting others, talking about others— even in Sunday school "prayer time"—or betraying a confidence.

Read James 3:1–12. What does James warn against?

According to James, if you want to be a teacher, what must you do?

If you want to disciple a younger woman, then you are about to take on a huge task. You must know how to keep another's confidence and not talk about what is discussed in private. Nothing hinders a relationship more than knowing you can't trust someone. Almost every week someone shares with me their struggles or hurts. I know more about the girls in our college group than even they realize. But, I would never share any of it with another person. I want my girls to trust me and know I am a safe person to confide in. Only then will I have an opportunity to speak truth into their lives and show them how God can and will rescue them. Gossiping or sharing what they've told me in secret will only hurt them, and eventually my ministry.

Where would you place yourself on the gossip continuum?

1		10
I never gossip and I'm rarely tempted to gossip.	————————	I can't keep my mouth shut— even if my life depended on it

If you are on the far left of the continuum, keep it up. Pray God would continue to give you opportunities to speak into others' lives. If you are on the far right, please pray God would get a hold of your mouth. Ask mature, godly women to hold you accountable. I even knew one woman who put a rubber band around her wrist. Every time she began to gossip, she gave herself a good pop. Ladies, we must do whatever it takes to stop our gossiping, slanderous mouths. Let's work on this together.

Not Addictive, Enslaved to Substances

"And don't get drunk with wine, which leads to reckless actions, but be filled by the Spirit" (Ephesians 5:18).

Besides the obvious, what comparison—between being filled with wine versus being filled with the Spirit—is Paul making?

In Ephesians 5:18, Paul makes a comparison between what it means to be controlled by the Holy Spirit versus being controlled or addicted to another substance. Self-control is a fruit of the Spirit, and it is imperative in the life of a believer (Gal. 5:22–23). Ladies, when you are enslaved to anything besides God, then you are not living a life of freedom and control. A Titus 2 woman is one who seeks to allow God to be *the* controlling factor in her life and resists the temptation to be controlled by any outside force.

What controls your life?

What changes do you need to make to allow the Holy Spirit to be *the* controlling factor in your life?

If you have a problem with addiction (whether its drugs, alcohol, or another substance), please get help. There are great Scripture-based programs, such as Celebrate Recovery, to help you. Find an accountability person to pray with you and over you. Don't fight the battle of addiction alone. God has people in your community, and maybe in your church, who will come alongside you to give you encouragement. You don't have to live in bondage to addiction (Gal. 5:1). Get help and get out! You won't be sorry.

Able to Teach

Well, I was tracking with you, but I'm out. God hasn't given me the gift of teaching, so I guess I'm disqualified to be a mentor. Nope! I'm not asking you to get up in front of a group of people and teach them, and neither is God. The Greek word translated "teach" doesn't mean to teach what is learned in a classroom setting. Instead, this word refers to a woman's "reverent behavior," which shows an example of a woman who is set apart.[32] Basically, Paul said that a disciple maker will teach by her example.

Why do you think it's more important to teach by example and not merely through words?

Describe someone you know who is a great teacher, but she/he has never formally taught a class.

This world is filled with all kinds of ungodliness. If you want to be exposed to filth, then turn on the television or your computer. It's much easier and more enticing to give into the world's influence than it is to fight it. Ladies, there are young women who need to know that it's OK to say no to the world. The lure to sin is constant, and we need older, mature women in the faith to stand up and model a life of godliness and self-control.

So there you have it. Those are the five qualifications to be a Titus 2 woman. Does the description fit your life? If not, then it needs to. Please make changes in your life so that you can step up and be obedient to God's command to disciple a spiritually younger woman. Don't disqualify yourself from being used by God to do incredible things for the kingdom. If it does describe you, I'm excited for you. Thank you for contributing to God's work in women's lives. Regardless of where you are in becoming or being a Titus 2 woman, prayerfully consider these questions.

 REST STOP: How does God want you to respond?

Is it past time for you to step up and lead younger women? What changes need to occur in your life so you can take on that role?

Who are you discipling or mentoring?

THE TITUS 2 CURRICULUM

Read Titus 2:3–5 again. We've talked about this before, but indulge me for a moment. Who is responsible for teaching younger women?

If you answered, "older women," then you are correct. I'm so glad you were paying attention in our last section. There is a good reason that Paul didn't command Titus to teach the younger women, but instead, gave that to the older women. Woman-to-woman discipleship has always been God's preferred method for discipleship because women learn best from other women. As we look at the curriculum for discipleship, you will see that it takes a woman to teach these things.

ಏ ಲ

Woman-to-woman discipleship has always been God's preferred method for discipleship because women learn best from other women.

ಏ ಲ

When you hear the word *discipleship*, what comes to your mind?

When considering discipleship, most women think of learning to study the Bible, learning to lead a Bible study, or learning how to walk through a difficult time with integrity. Though all of these are good things that are vital to a Christian's growth, Paul doesn't mention any of these. Instead, Paul focuses on a woman's character and her home life. So, let's look at our curriculum for discipleship.

Love Their Husband and Children

What? Learning to study the Bible and pray isn't the first thing on the list? Nope! Paul immediately addresses the family relationship. A woman's top priority should be her family and her home, so naturally, this is a good place to start.

If you were writing this letter, what would you have said is the top priority in discipleship?

Look back at week 3. What type of love was a man to demonstrate to his wife?

God asks husbands to love their wives with an *agapē* — Godlike—love. However, Paul uses another type of love when addressing wives. He uses the Greek word *philandros* to explain the type of love a woman is to have toward her husband.

What English word do you see rooted in *philandros*?

What does a philanthropist do?

Philandros is rooted in the Greek word *phileō*, meaning "brotherly love or affection."[33] The English word *philanthropy* or *philanthropist* also comes from this word. A *phileō* type of love calls for a love and respect that goes with making a house a home. In using the word "brotherly love," Paul reminds us that our husbands need us to come alongside them and be their helper and friend.[34] When life gets tough—and it will—our husbands need us to show care, generosity, and humility.

My husband is a man's man. Before he went into full-time ministry, he was a football coach for ten years. He was a lineman in college, so he's tall and sturdy. But, he has one of the most caring hearts of anyone I know. Me … well, let's just say that when it comes to being merciful or compassionate, I've scored a zero—yes a zero—on a spiritual inventory test. So compassion isn't my thing. However, whenever my husband is struggling and needs his wife's support and love, I need to give it to him. Therefore, I'm thankful for a friend who is full of mercy and compassion who's modeled to me what true compassion should look like in a marriage. She's helped me and prayed for me as I've struggled to exercise it. I may have to work at it, but after five years of marriage, I'm getting better. As I practice *phileō* love toward my husband, our marriage grows stronger and our love grows deeper.

Does compassion come easy for you? If so, how can you use that to help a younger wife and/or mother in her family life?

If compassion doesn't come easy for you, do you know women who can come alongside you and help you learn it?

Self-controlled

We've seen this word before. Yep, it was in the qualifications of a Titus 2 woman. Self-control is almost nonexistent in our culture. If we want something, we take it. We are an overindulged society, and the bigger the better. The term "self-control" can also be described as being sensible or discreet. As an independent woman, it is difficult to not be overbearing, tactless, and to do things my way. Though there is nothing sinful about a strong woman who is firm in her convictions, a mature woman knows when to balance strength with tact. Paul encourages the older women in the faith to teach and model discretion (self-control) to the younger women in the faith.

ᐧᐧ ᐧᐧ

Though there is nothing sinful about a strong woman who is firm in her convictions, a mature woman knows when to balance strength with tact.

ᐧᐧ ᐧᐧ

There are appropriate times to speak and appropriate times to keep your mouth shut. There are appropriate times to act with swiftness on an issue, and there are appropriate times to wait. Younger women need to learn and understand the difference between when and how to act.

Does self-control come easily for you, or is it something you struggle with?

How can you change things in your life to grow in this area? What could God be asking you to give up to become more self-controlled in your life?

Pure

Read Matthew 5:8. Who is considered blessed? What will they inherit?

The third part of the Titus 2 curriculum is purity. Purity can mean a lot of things, but in this passage Paul is specifically referring to sexual purity. Ladies, sexual purity in and outside the marriage relationship is crucial to the life of a Christ follower. Sexual purity is more than just not physically cheating on your husband; it also involves being pure in your thoughts and emotions (Matt. 5:27–30). Did you know that women are more likely to fall into an emotional affair before having a physical affair? I've seen it happen more than I like to admit. Therefore, we must be careful with what we read (including Christian romance novels), what we watch on television, look at on the computer, and what conversations we entertain with friends and coworkers. Did you also know that pornography is a growing trend among women? In talking with my students, I've had several of them admit to me that they struggle with porn or they have Christian friends who struggle with it. Ladies, Satan is out to destroy us through impurity. Let's fight him with everything in us.

If you are caught in the clutches of pornography, or any other sexual sin, check out this article.[35] Just go to the notes section of the study to find the website and title. Know I am praying for you. You aren't alone in your struggle.

 REST STOP: How has sexual impurity affected your life or the life of a friend? (You don't have to share that with the group.)

Offer a prayer to God of commitment or recommitment to purity.

Workers at Home

Paul said that older women are to model the art of homemaking to the younger women. The art of homemaking is a lost talent in America, but one that is so vital to the growth and nurture of families. Dorothy Patterson has a great commentary on what happens when moms fail to make home the priority.

> Bearing a new liberated identity, many women have devoted themselves to ambitious busyness everywhere but the home. They are enmeshed in overwhelming volunteerism to achieve accolades and recognition in the community, or they are surrogate wives and mothers to hatching

professional pursuits that promise power and pocketbook. Instead of encouraging adolescents to cut the apron strings of mother and venture out into society, we are begging mother not to cut the apron strings on their babies and catapult them prematurely into a menacing world![36]

In recent years, there has been a slow return of younger women into the home. I get to stay home with my children, and I have friends who are making the same decision. When Paul wrote this letter, the home was the central focus as a source of hospitality and a place to gather with friends. Therefore, he was encouraging women to use their homes as a place for hospitality, ministry, and the center for all activity.[37] Who wouldn't want to be in a home that was inviting? How would your home life be different if you used your home for ministry? Think of the conversations you could have with a hurting woman as she sat on your couch, drank coffee, and shared with you her struggles. Think of the influence you, as a mother, could have on your children and their friends as you made an afternoon snack for them. Think of the lack of stress in your home when you are already there to greet your husband and children as they return home from work or school. Your world, and your family's world, could look a lot different.

Over the last year, I've come to understand the importance of making my home my top priority. Before you get any ideas, I am not your "creative, Suzy homemaker." My grandmother always told me, "If you can read, then you can cook," so I took her advice. I rarely cook anything without a recipe in front of me. And any "creative" idea for my home comes from Pinterest or my sister-in-loves—all three are creative geniuses. Learning to cook, keep a house, and raise my children has been difficult for me. But it's also been refreshing. While my girls nap, I've learned that it is OK to have women, or my college girls, into our home. I may be in the middle of eating lunch or preparing supper, but they don't seem to mind. Some of my favorite times of ministry have happened between 1:00 and 3:00 in the afternoon. I've realized that God doesn't want to limit the educational or creative pursuits of a woman. Instead, God desires for women to use their home as a basis and catalyst for ministry.

Does the thought of using your home for ministry excite or terrify you?

List one way, big or small, that you can use your home as a catalyst for ministry.

Kindhearted

A woman who seeks to be a Titus 2 woman must be kind and teach others how to be kind. Kindness is one of the demonstrations of the fruit of the Spirit laid out in Galatians 5:22–23. Kindness goes deeper than being nice because it is a state of the heart and not dependent upon another's actions. It is difficult to be kind in a harsh world, and older women in the faith need to model kindness to the younger women.

Would people characterize you as kind or callous?

When you speak, do you speak with kindness, or do you tend to give people a piece of your mind?

Let's seek to be women who are kind to others. We can't teach kindness if we are impatient or intolerant of others. When we are tempted to respond in anger or with a harsh word, let's commit to stop, think about our attitude, and then respond in a manner that would bring God glory.

Submission to Your Husband

There it is again—that word *submission*. Yes, older women are to teach and model what it means to be submissive to a husband. Again, Paul uses the Greek word *hupotassō* to define submission. We have already discussed the importance of a wife coming under her husband's authority as the leader of their home, so we won't belabor the issue. However, it's important for us to realize that we can't teach what we don't practice. God knew that young wives (and even older wives) would struggle with submission, so He asked the spiritually mature women to model and teach submission to the spiritually immature women.

Remember my introduction when I told you about my overseas supervisors and their marriage? Though I wasn't married, the wife demonstrated to me that submission shouldn't be a scary thing. She also showed me that I could be a strong woman *and* a submissive wife. I'm human, so I still struggle, but I know I have older, more mature women who will be there to help me learn how to come under my husband's authority.

Share a time when a spiritually mature woman helped you in your marriage.

If you aren't married, do you have marriages that you look up to? What makes them so special?

The Titus 2 curriculum may not be what you thought it would be. To be honest with you, it's a lot easier to teach a woman how to read and study her Bible or to pray than it is to teach her how to love her husband, be pure, be self-controlled, and submissive. If you truly want to teach what is laid out in this passage, then you have to get your hands dirty. You have to do life with a younger woman and allow her to see your strengths, weaknesses, failures, and accomplishments. This is way more intimidating than getting up in front of a class, teaching a lesson, and then going home. Life-on-life and woman-to-woman discipleship is what the church needs. It needs people like you and me to step up and take responsibility for the young women in our lives. If we refuse to be obedient to disciple others, then God gives us a warning—and you don't want to mess with God.

> 𝕾𝕮𝕽
>
> *If you truly want to teach what is laid out in this passage, then you have to get your hands dirty. You have to do life with a younger woman and allow her to see your strengths, weaknesses, failures, and accomplishments.*
>
> 𝕾𝕮𝕽

WARNING: ALL HANDS ON DECK

Read Titus 2:5. What is the warning Paul gives to women who refuse to disciple younger women?

Ladies, when we don't take discipleship seriously, then God's Word is at stake. Paul says spiritually mature women were to teach spiritually immature women the above curriculum so that "God's message will not be slandered" (Titus 2:5). *Blasphēmeō* is the Greek word translated "slandered" in the HCSB.

Look at *blasphēmeō*. Do you see an English word embedded in it?

This is where we get our English word "blasphemy." *Blasphēmeō* means "to speak against God so that you cast through or make null and void God's word and His truths."[38]

Read Luke 12:10. What does this verse say?

What happens to someone who speaks against the Holy Spirit?

In case you were wondering, the same Greek word is used in this verse. Ladies, God is jealous of His name and His glory (Exod. 34:13–14). Therefore, it is imperative that we obey God's commands to be self-controlled, pure, kind, submissive, and so on. This is a scary thought: Disobedience to these commands can confuse non-Christians into assuming that Jesus doesn't change a person's heart and behavior, but instead causes them to remain the same. Ladies, as a nineteen-year-old young woman, Jesus reached down and saved me. He pulled me out of a heap of sin and gave me peace, comfort, and freedom that I had never experienced. I was trapped in sin, but now I am free. I was living in constant fear, but now I have peace and hope. I was drowning in condemnation, but God took away my shame and lifted up my face. Because of the blood of Jesus, I am who I am. I want other women to know that He can and will do the same for them. I want my life to reflect what Jesus did in my heart. Ladies, I don't want to blaspheme my precious Savior's name or reputation. Therefore, I must speak out. I must teach. And, I must take a younger woman and show her what God can do in and through her.

What about you? Does your life reflect the Titus 2 woman?

REST STOP: If you stood before God today, would He find you as a faithful disciple? If not, what needs to change in your life?

Ladies, God is serious about discipleship. Younger women are looking to older women to model to them what a godly woman looks like in a godless world. They need us to step up and live life with them. Are you willing? Would you at least consider it? Is there a woman you can disciple? If so, what's stopping you from doing it? I certainly don't want to be guilty of blaspheming God's name. Instead, my prayer is that I would obey the Titus 2 model of discipleship. I will be praying the same for you. We have much to teach, so let's get busy teaching.

Week 5

DRIVERS BEWARE:
INTERPRETING DIFFICULT PASSAGES

Almost four years ago my husband and I went on a three-week road trip. He wanted me to meet some of his relatives from Texas and Colorado, and I wanted him to meet my best friend, who lives in Nebraska. We also wanted to escape the Louisiana summer and anywhere sounded, and felt, better than here. So we piled in the car, along with our three-month-old daughter—oh, I didn't mention we did this with an infant?—and started out on our journey.

Once we got into Colorado, I began to see signs that read: "Drivers Beware: Steep Grade." Louisiana doesn't have mountains—we have swamps—so this was a new one for me. I was pretty sure what "steep grade" meant (the signs provided pictures), but I didn't understand their significance. A few moments later, I discovered exactly what they meant. There was an 18-wheeler who had lost control of his brakes and had slammed into the side of the mountain. Thankfully, he made it to one of the runaway truck ramps, and he didn't appear to be injured.

Interpreting difficult passages can be a lot like driving in the Colorado mountains. There are a lot of twists and turns, and it's very easy to lose your brakes and plow headlong into disaster.

Before you know it, you can be carried away by something that "sounds" right, but it isn't theologically correct.

This week we will look at three different difficult passages that are often debated in theological circles. If you have a tendency to do your study in one day, please try to avoid doing that this week. There is a lot of information to cover. So, if you wait until the last minute to do it, you will get bogged down and overwhelmed. Take the week slow, read each passage carefully, and you will get it. I'm praying for you this week.

BIBLICAL WHAT?

I want to introduce you to a very big seminary word ... biblical hermeneutics (pronounced: her-men-new-tics). *Hermeneutics* simply means "the art or process of interpreting." Therefore, *biblical hermeneutics* means the art or process of interpreting the Bible. (See, it's not all that complicated. And now you have a word you can use to impress your friends.) Ladies, God's Word is inspired by God, timeless (it will endure through the ages), inerrant (without error), authoritative, and sufficient (it contains all one needs to live a life of godliness).[39] Therefore, as we look at these three passages this week, we will use different parts of Scripture to gain a fuller understanding of each passage.

When interpreting difficult or unclear passages, that upon first glance seem to contradict other parts of Scripture, you must follow a set of hermeneutical guidelines. Just as that "runaway truck ramp" protected drivers if and when they lost control, these hermeneutical guidelines can help you tackle the twists and turns that accompany understanding the truth of God's Word. We will follow four hermeneutical guidelines as we look at this week's passages.

- **We must come to the Scriptures with a humble, teachable spirit.** Oftentimes, our fallen nature wants to make the Bible say what we want it to say. When Scripture challenges our culture, it is easier to agree with the culture than conform ourselves to God's Word. So we don't ever want to approach God's word with any preconceived ideas and assume we have it all together. God wants to speak to us, but we must approach Him with our hearts ready to learn.

- **We must realize that God doesn't want to hide or prevent us from knowing Him through His Word.** God has left us with His Spirit and His Word to be the "lamp for my feet and a light on my path" (Ps. 119:105). Therefore, we can rest assured that God, through the Holy Spirit, desires to give clarity to His people. Trust Him for clarity.

- **We must interpret difficult passages in light of clear passages**. God never contradicts Himself. Therefore, when there is an apparent conflict between two passages, then the problem resides with us and not the Scripture itself. It is our responsibility to continue working through the Scripture passage until clarity is achieved. So, when things get tough, don't give up.

- **We must consider the Bible in its entirety.**[40] When we don't understand portions of Scripture, it is easier to ignore them as not relevant in today's culture, isolate them from the rest of Scripture, or throw the passage out as not authoritative or useless. Scripture interprets Scripture; therefore, the entire Word of God must be considered.

SPEECHLESS SUBMISSION?

"As in all the churches of the saints, the women should be silent in the churches, for they are not permitted to speak, but should be submissive, as the law also says. And if they want to learn something, they should ask their own husbands at home, for it is disgraceful for a woman to speak in the church meeting" (1 Cor. 14:33b–35).

React to this passage. What do you think Paul is saying to us in the twenty-first century?

The Context Matters

When you pick up a book to read, where do you start? You always begin at the beginning. However, we are all guilty of picking up the Bible, turning to a random chapter, and then reading it. If you do this with 1 Corinthians 14:33–35, then this passage seems antiwomen and sexist. Therefore, before any judgments are made, we will consider the context of the text.

In 1 Corinthians 12, Paul gives a list of spiritual gifts that are offered to both men and women. He also says that all believers are part of Christ's body and are one in Christ. Paul uses examples from our physical bodies to teach a spiritual truth; every member of Christ's body is needed and valuable. No one would ever tell her foot or ear that they are not needed. When we have a pain in one part of our body, then the rest of our body suffers. The same is true with the body of Christ, the church.

In chapter 13, Paul shows the motivation for exercising your gift. First Corinthians 13 is the famous "love chapter." It is often used in marriage ceremonies, which is appropriate. But marriage is not the central focus of this passage. Paul tells the Corinthian church that they should exercise their spiritual gifts—whether it is prophecy, speaking in tongues, healing, faith, or interpreting of tongues—in an attitude of love. This truth also applies to us. Your spiritual gift is not better than mine and vice versa. We are all members of Christ's body, and we are all needed in the kingdom of God.

In chapter 14, Paul begins to highlight the differences between prophecy and speaking in tongues. He tells them that they should desire to prophesy instead of speak in tongues because prophesying is done for the edification or "building up" of the body of Christ. He then gives regulations for speaking in tongues, stating that if one speaks in an unknown tongue, then there must be an interpreter present. The Corinthians' worship services had become loud and disorderly because everyone was speaking over everyone else. No one knew what was going on and certainly not much scriptural teaching was understood. It is within this section that Paul makes the claim; "women should be silent in the churches, for they are not permitted to speak, but should be submissive, as the law also says" (1 Cor. 14:34).

In chapter 15, Paul seems to move to another question the church of Corinth asked him. They obviously asked him about Jesus' resurrection because chapter 15 is an explanation on the importance of Christ's resurrection from the dead. Remember, both First and Second Corinthians are letters written to a particular church, in a particular culture, and answering specific questions. We do not have a copy of the letter that was written to Paul, but we do have his response to those questions.

What do you think we miss when we pick up the Bible, turn to a random chapter, and then begin reading?

Do you think this practice aids in our misunderstanding and misuse of Scripture? Why or why not?

Does Paul Really Mean Silent Submission?

The command for women's silence is a seemingly strange command. You may be thinking, "Is Paul really saying that women are not to utter a sound in church, but instead ask their husbands at home? How is a single woman, who has no husband, to gain clarity on a spiritual truth? Why does Paul say that it is 'shameful' for a woman to speak in church? That seems a bit harsh." Let's look at these questions in light of the hermeneutical guidelines we set up at the beginning of this week. I want you to first pray and ask God to reveal "the deep and hidden things" and to bring to light what seems to be hidden (Dan. 2:22).

What is clear about this passage of Scripture?

First, there was disorder in the church service. In First Corinthians 14:27–33a, Paul addresses that disorder by giving them guidelines to use. Regarding speaking in tongues, Paul exhorts them to have at most three people who exercise that gift. After each person speaks in a tongue, then there must be someone present to interpret what was said. The purpose of a worship service is not to edify self but to edify and lift up Jesus. Therefore, God desires for each person to exercise her spiritual gift in an orderly fashion. I think we can all learn a thing or two from that truth. Worship is about Jesus, not me!

Secondly, this passage encourages women to learn spiritual truths (v. 35). Women in the first century were seen as incapable of learning anything, especially theological truths; yet, Paul encourages women to ask questions and seek answers to those questions. Paul also affirms the spiritual leadership of the husband. A husband should know the Scriptures well enough to be able to instruct his wife. Also, a wife should know the Scriptures in order to intelligently ask questions of her husband.[41]

Finally, this passage shows that Paul considers the gift of prophecy more beneficial to the body than speaking in tongues. He does not discount the gift of tongues, but he does give guidelines for its use.

What other clear truths did you see in 1 Corinthians 14?

What is confusing about this passage?

There is one main problem with this passage. First Corinthians 14:33–35 seems to contradict 1 Corinthians 11:5. First Corinthians 11:5 says, "But every woman who prays or prophesies with her head uncovered dishonors her head, since that is one and the same as having her head shaved." In this verse Paul gives guidelines for women speaking in church, but in 1 Corinthians 14:34–35, Paul seems to completely forbid women to speak in church. Therefore, either the Bible explicitly contradicts itself, or there must be an alternative interpretation. The following examples are scholars' attempt at bringing reconciliation to 1 Corinthians 11:5 and 1 Corinthians 14:34–35.

Egalitarian Position

Sometimes it's easier to decipher truth when we first discover what is not truth. Let's first consider the evangelical feminist interpretation. For years, feminist scholars tried to explain away 1 Corinthians 14:33–35. In recent years, one egalitarian scholar continued the debate that verses 34–35 were not original to Paul's letter, but they were added into the text at a later date.[42] He said that Paul would not agree that women are to remain silent because he gives women permission to speak in other parts of Scripture. However, there is one problem with this objection. Over and over again, scholars have proved that 1 Corinthians 14:33–35 are in every manuscript that has been discovered. They are located either where most English readers find them (after verse 33), or they are located after verse 40.[43]

Another evangelical feminist interpretation is that the women were either being too noisy or they were uneducated. Therefore, in order to prevent uneducated women from causing confusion by teaching heresy in the church, Paul tells them to remain silent.[44] This sounds good to us who are educated because it would mean the command is for the Corinthian women only, and it does not pertain to women in the twenty-first century. But, there is no evidence in this text or outside this text to prove that Paul commands women to be silent because of their lack of education or their noisy disposition.[45]

Complementarian Position

Another possible explanation for verses 34–35 is that the women in Corinth were embarrassing their husbands by questioning their husbands' prophecies. As a result, they were seeking to undermine their husbands' authority. This argument states that Paul demands for these women to restrict their questioning of their husbands to their home.[46]

Do any (or all) of these interpretations resonate with you? Why or why not?

There are other speculations for the meaning of these verses (whole books have been written to explain these verses), but we are just looking at some of the most common objections. We have looked at several ways this verse brings confusion. There is one more hermeneutical guideline we need to consider. How do verses 34–35 fit in with the rest of 1 Corinthians and with the rest of Scripture?

How does this passage and its interpretation fit in with the rest of Scripture?

In verses 29–33, Paul gives guidelines on speaking prophecy. He says that they are to take turns prophesying, and two people are not to speak at one time. After each person has spoken, then there should be a time where the spoken prophecy is evaluated by those present (v. 29). The word *evaluate* is translated "pass judgment or judge" in other Bible translations.[47] When someone weighed or evaluated a spoken prophecy then they did so to determine whether or not it was valid and consistent with the teachings of Jesus.[48] Therefore, it was more of a teaching role instead of a participatory role. It is after the instruction of evaluating prophesies that Paul then states "women should be silent in the churches."

The evaluation of another's prophecy caused a problem for women, especially wives. Wives are under their husband's authority and spiritual leadership, and a wife questioning her husband in the public assembly would be undermining his authority as her spiritual leader.[49] So, what is Paul's solution? He told the women, if they had a question, they were to ask their husbands at home. It's not that Paul wanted to prevent a woman from questioning her husband's prophecy, but he instructed the wives to do it in the privacy of their home.

Why would Paul allow a woman to prophesy in the church (1 Cor. 11:5) but forbid her to interpret prophecies in church? Teaching and prophecy are viewed as two different gifts. The Bible seems to indicate that prophecy occurs after someone has a "revelation" from God, so it is more spontaneous (1 Cor. 14:30–31). However, in the New Testament, the term "teaching" has a more formal undertone. It means the explaining of

Scripture and then teaching the application of Scripture. If you examine other scripture passages, it appears that teaching holds more influence than prophecy.[50] James 3:1 says, "Not many should become teachers, my brothers, knowing that we will receive a stricter judgment." Scripture also says that teaching—not prophesying—is one of the qualifications of an overseer/elder in the church (1 Tim. 3:2). Therefore, when an individual "evaluates" a prophecy, then he or she explains the meaning of that prophecy, taking on more of a teaching role.[51] It is at the point of "weighing" (teaching) prophecies that Paul commands women to be silent. (The next passage deals with women teaching men, so you will gain a better understanding of why this interpretation is important.)

I just gave you, in a few paragraphs, what I spent several seminary classes and hours studying. What is one thing you question about this interpretation?

Does this interpretation make sense to you?

Is this interpretation consistent with the rest of Scripture?

Based on 1 Timothy 2:11–12, this interpretation is consistent with the rest of Scripture. First Timothy 2:12 says that a woman is not to "teach or to have authority over a man." (We will look more in depth at these verses in the next section, so I will not spend time on them here.) In 1 Corinthians 14:34–35, Paul is being consistent with Scripture's teaching on male headship and male leadership within the church. In verse 34,

Paul refers back to the Law. The Law (meaning the Law of Moses—found in Exodus–Deuteronomy) is the foundation for male leadership, and it determined a distinction between the roles of men and women.[52] In 1 Corinthians 14:34–35, Paul encourages women to seek answers to the questions they have when people prophesied, but he limited it to the home. He commanded women to be silent in the weighing of prophecies so they would not bring shame upon themselves or their husbands for questioning him in the public assembly. Remember, God is concerned with order, and a woman explaining, teaching, and instructing men, particularly her husband, in public was not permitted.[53]

How would you explain this interpretation to a friend?

How can you be obedient to 1 Corinthians 14:33–35 without taking the command "too far"—meaning women are forbidden to *ever* speak in worship services?

Good work today! Scripture interpretation is hard work and not for the fainthearted. I'm glad you stuck with it. Even if you are still trying to wrap your mind around all the objections and interpretations, my prayer is that you keep the main thing in front of you: Jesus wants you to know Him and His Word. Take a break, and I will see you back tomorrow.

WHO HAS THE AUTHORITY?

I'm so glad you came back. Do you see your brain, and most importantly your faith, growing? God is working in you, so keep it up. Because of your hard work yesterday, 1 Timothy 2:9–15 may be a little easier to grasp. Don't forget to pray and ask God to give you His supernatural understanding and discernment. Let's get to work.

> *Also, the women are to dress themselves in modest clothing, with decency and good sense, not with elaborate hairstyles, gold, pearls, or expensive apparel, but with good works, as is proper for women who affirm that they worship God. A woman should learn in silence with full submission. I do not allow a woman to teach or to have authority over a man; instead, she is to be silent. For Adam was created first, then Eve. And Adam was not deceived, but the woman was deceived and transgressed. But she will be saved through childbearing, if she continues in faith, love, and holiness, with good judgment. (1 Timothy 2:9–15)*

What are some things in this passage that bother you? To what do you give a hearty "Amen"?

Based on yesterday's interpretation, do you have some ideas on why God would give us this command?

Context Matters

The content of 1 Timothy 2:9–15 almost mirrors that of 1 Corinthian 14:34–35, but its context is different. First and 2 Timothy are letters that Paul wrote to Timothy, his son in the faith. Paul was discipling this young pastor, and his letters were written to encourage Timothy and give him guidance on how to lead a church. If God has given you the opportunity to mentor another woman, make sure you're speaking truth into her life and encourage her to stand firm in the faith. Don't ever overlook the impact your words have on her life.

In chapter 1, Paul warns Timothy about people who would come in and teach a doctrine that goes against Scripture and the things that Timothy had learned from Paul. He also told Timothy to stay in Ephesus so he could "instruct certain people not to teach different doctrine or to pay attention to myths and endless genealogies" (1 Tim 1:3–4). Paul, then, gives Timothy a reminder of the gospel message that he had taught him: "Christ Jesus came into the world to save sinners" (1 Tim 1:15). Paul ends the first chapter encouraging Timothy to continue to fight the false doctrines that some were trying to teach.

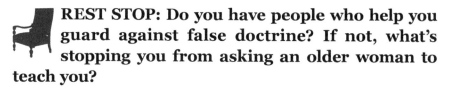

REST STOP: Do you have people who help you guard against false doctrine? If not, what's stopping you from asking an older woman to teach you?

In chapter 2, Paul begins to give instruction on people within the church. He tells Timothy to pray for all people, especially those who are in positions of authority. He then gives instructions on how men and women are to pray and conduct themselves. He tells men to pray without "anger or argument," and then Paul instructs women to exhibit modesty and self-control (vv. 8–9). It is within this chapter that Paul tells women to "learn in silence" (v. 11). He also says he does not "allow a woman to teach or to have authority over a man" (v. 12). Paul ends the chapter by giving an odd and confusing commentary on Adam and Eve.

In chapter 3, Paul gives instructions for the offices of the church. He lists the qualifications for men who desire to be overseers or deacons within the church. He also gives a list of qualifications for deacons' wives. Chapter 3 ends with Paul telling Timothy how Christians, and especially Christian leaders, should behave. In chapter 4, Paul goes back to explaining the different myths and false doctrines that could infiltrate the church. According to First Timothy 4, some of the false teaching that was rampant in the church of Ephesus included abstinence from certain foods (1 Tim. 4:3), an abstinence from marriage (1 Tim. 4:3; 5:14–15), and maybe an abstinence from sex. Paul warns Timothy against these doctrines and tells him to teach and preach the truth of God that he learned from Paul.

Women and Teaching Authority

First Timothy 2:9–15 is a passage that has stirred up a lot of controversy in recent years. There have been whole books written on these seven verses, so we will only begin to scratch the surface of its meaning. If egalitarians can disprove, reinterpret, or dismiss these verses, then the pastorate and other forms of authority within the church are opened to women. We will see that egalitarians don't think these verses can be taken at face value (meaning there is an alternative interpretation), but complementarians believe these verses teach a clear command from Scripture.

These are some questions we will seek to answer. Does Paul really command a woman to not teach a man? Is this command only Paul's preference but not a command from God? Was this command binding only to the church of Ephesus, or does it still stand today? As with the previous passage, we will use the hermeneutical guidelines presented at the beginning of the week to help us answer these questions.

What is clear about this passage of Scripture?

There are several commands that are clear in this passage. First, Christians are to pray for their leaders and those who are in authority over them (v. 2). This means that we must pray for our president, our pastor, our boss at work, and anyone else who may hold a position of authority. Secondly, God desires for all people to come to a saving knowledge of Jesus (v. 4). He is the atoning sacrifice for our sin, and God desires for none to perish and live apart from Him. Thirdly, Paul encourages the men to cease their fighting with each other and to live in peace instead of anger (v. 8). Men are not the only ones who struggle with anger, but in this passage Paul specifically points out men.

The last clear command deals with a woman's clothing choices. Paul encourages the women to dress modestly and to have "decency and good sense" in their choice of clothing. I'm going to take a little detour and address the issue of modesty. I realize that modesty can be in the eyes of the beholder, but I also know that we, as women, struggle with modesty and understanding its effect on men.

In First Timothy 2:9–10, Paul makes a comparison between modest dress and godliness. There are several interpretations of these verses, and we won't get into them here. Some religious sects have gone so far in their interpretation as to require women to cover up every part of their body, including their face. Know that Paul is not asking women to wear a certain style of clothing or to be ashamed of their bodies. God made our bodies, and He made them beautiful. Instead Paul says that a woman's focus should not be *merely* on her outward appearance ("elaborate hairstyles, gold, pearls, or expensive apparel"). Ladies, if we are giving more attention to our outward appearance instead of our relationship with Jesus, then we have our priorities mixed up.

Yes, we are to be good stewards of our body—which Scripture calls the "temple of the Holy Spirit"—but we are to use our temple to bring honor and glory to God and not attention to ourselves (1 Cor. 6:19). (Please don't confuse modesty with forbidding clothing styles. You can take almost any "in style" look and make it modest *and* cute. Dress cute. But, dress cute for God's glory.) I have often wondered how God-centered and God-focused our churches would be if we put as much focus on our spiritual life as we do our outward appearance. A woman who seeks to glorify God will not dress immodestly because she will exhibit self-control in her dressing. OK, I'm finished with my soap box.

Ladies, if we are giving more attention to our outward appearance instead of our relationship with Jesus, then we have our priorities mixed up.

REST STOP: Do you dress to please God or to please others?

Is there anything in your closet that you need to throw away? Are you willing to make a change toward modesty?

What is confusing about this passage of Scripture?

There are several confusing concepts in 1 Timothy 2:11–15. First, Paul again seems to single out women as inferior to men. He tells them to "learn in silence with full submission" (v. 11). He then forbids a woman "to teach or to have authority over a man" (v. 12). Secondly, Paul says that Eve was the one deceived, and that is the reason that women should not teach men. Finally, Paul gives a confusing commentary on Adam and Eve. Paul seems to insinuate that women have their salvation in childbearing. So, does this mean that a single lady or a woman who does not have a child cannot be saved? The following are scholars' attempts at explaining and interpreting this passage.

Egalitarian Interpretation

Let's first look at the evangelical feminist view of these verses. I'm going to single out two main theologians who have written extensively on 1 Timothy 2:9–15. For example, Richard and Catherine Kroeger wrote an entire book dedicated to this passage. Their main thesis states, "Our purpose is to maintain on the basis of Scripture that both men and women are equally called to commitment and service, *wherever* and *however* God may lead" (emphasis added).[54] They form their argument around the presumption that the women in the church of Ephesus were teaching heresy, namely that Eve was the one who was created first.[55] Therefore, Paul commands them to stop. The writers then seek ancient material and alternative suggestions for the interpretation of these verses in order to prove that women were teaching heresy.

The Kroegers' main objection to the complementarian view is the interpretation of the phrase "to have authority over." They accuse traditional interpreters of only presenting one interpretation of the Greek word *authentein*, which is translated in the KJV as "to usurp authority over."[56] (*Authentein* is a *hapax legomenon*, meaning it is only used once in the New Testament.) The Kroegers give an alternative meaning for the word *authentein*. They say the word can also be translated, "I do not allow a woman to teach nor *to proclaim herself author of a man*" (emphasis added).[57] The writers believe that Paul warned women to stop repeating the heretical teaching that woman were the authors or originators of men—meaning Eve was created first. The Kroegers conclude their interpretation of verse 12 by stating that Paul's actual meaning of the command, "I do not allow a woman to teach or to have authority over a man" should actually be translated "I do not permit woman to teach or to represent herself as originator of man but she is to be in conformity [with the Scriptures]."[58] In the Kroegers' interpretation, a woman is *not* forbidden to teach men or to have authority over them. Instead, women are cautioned against teaching heresy. As long as a woman is not teaching heresy, then she is given the freedom to teach both men and women.

I just gave you a lot of information. Go back and reread it and then put it in your own words. What is the Kroegers' interpretation of 2 Timothy 2:11–15?

There are two main problems with the Kroegers' interpretation. First, in the church of Ephesus, only men are accused of teaching heresy (1 Tim. 1:20; 2 Tim. 2:17–18).[59] It is true that the theme of First and Second Timothy is Paul's warning against false teachers or heresy, but women were not the ones involved in this teaching. Instead, women are accused of being "idlers, gossips and busybodies" (1 Tim. 5:13). Though a gossip can and does retell what might not be truth, a gossip is not defined in Scripture as a false teacher.

Secondly, the Kroegers have no proof the Ephesian women were teaching that Eve was created first. Actually, there is no proof from any of the first-century writers that this teaching was pervasive in the New Testament period. Instead, they have to seek other writers and other time periods for this reference. Yet, even those sources do not hold up to scholarly analysis. The Kroegers misinterpret the historical facts about Ephesus and paint a false picture of the culture of Ephesus.[60] Therefore, the interpretation based on heresy and a redefinition of the phrase "to exercise authority over" should be dismissed.

Another egalitarian argument is that the Ephesian women were not as educated as the men. Therefore, they were to remain silent and not teach men.[61] One of the scholars of this interpretation is Gilbert Bilezikian (pronounced Bael-zi-kan). To further emphasis this point, Bilezikian writes the phrase "I do not permit" should actually be translated "I do not permit *now* a woman to teach."[62] (Emphasis in original text.) He goes on to argue that when these women were well versed and educated in the things of God, then Paul would remove the restriction on women. He also cautions church leaders to only put in positions of authority those women who are mature in their faith and capable of teaching. Since we now live in a society where women are educated, the command for women to not teach men is no longer valid.

This is a very popular interpretation of 1 Timothy 2:11–15. What is appealing about it?

Do you see where there could be some issues with it?

There are a couple of problems with Bilezikian's interpretation. First, the passage does not say that women are less educated than men. It does say that Eve was deceived, "and became a transgressor." But it does not mean that all women, in every location, are deceived and lack biblical understanding. Actually, in the Greek and Roman world, both girls and boys had access to a basic education, which included reading and writing.

Another problem with this interpretation is that Scripture shows women in Ephesus who were capable of teaching.[63] In Acts 18:24–28, Luke says Priscilla, a woman—along with her husband, Aquila—explained to Apollos "the way of God to him more accurately" (v. 26). Priscilla and Aquila learned from Paul and were certainly capable of standing up against false teachers. But, in the public assembly, God, through Paul, commands for all women to "not teach or to have authority over a man."

Complementarian Interpretation

Complementarians—including me—teach women are to have *restricted* leadership within the church. Paul clearly says that a woman is not to "teach or to have authority over a man," which limits women in certain church roles. But, how did we come to this conclusion?

Before we move forward, I would like to make one clarification on First Timothy 2:11–15. First and 2 Timothy are written to give instructions on life within the family and especially within the church. There have been conservative pastors and teachers who have mistakenly hurt women who held leadership positions in a secular setting by stating these women were undermining Scriptures' authority by teaching men. This passage is not addressing women who are CEOs of a corporation, team leaders of a work group, or women professors teaching math at a university. It also doesn't mean that men can't learn anything from women. A man who closes his ears to anything a woman might say is prideful and not in step with God's heart. This passage specifically addresses the church assembly and should be interpreted in light of that fact.[64]

How does this passage and its interpretation fit in with the rest of Scripture?

First Timothy 2:11–15 is in harmony with the Scriptures' teaching of male headship and leadership. Paul first tells women to "learn in silence with full submission" (v. 11). We have already noted this fact, but the Jewish culture did not encourage women to learn spiritual truths. Therefore, in verse 11 Paul is actually encouraging women to learn, and he tells women how they should learn. Some scholars object to this verse based on the phrase "learn in silence." Their objection stems from the misunderstanding that 1 Timothy 2:11 teaches that women are to remain absolutely quiet in worship. But, you need only flip back a few pages in Scripture to discover that Paul has already given women the freedom to speak in the public assembly (1 Cor. 11:5). When you look at the Greek word for "quiet," it does not mean an absence of words. Instead, Paul is referring to a woman's "attitude and demeanor of 'quietness.'"[65] How can we learn anything if we don't stay quiet long enough to hear what is being taught? How can we learn if our hearts are not ready to submit to God's teaching? Therefore, this verse can be understood as God commanding women to learn with a teachable heart and spirit, submitting to the male leadership of the church.[66]

Have you ever approached Scripture or a worship service with an unteachable spirit? How much did God teach you?

In verse 12, Paul says, "I do not allow a woman to teach or to have authority over a man." Some evangelical feminist scholars note the tense in which Paul says, "I do not allow." Paul uses the Greek present tense, which means he was addressing a certain situation in the church of Ephesus. These scholars use the Greek language as an example to argue that this is not a binding command but a command that was given specifically to the church of Ephesus and to a particular situation.[67]

This argument sounds good and feasible, but in verses 13–15 Paul appeals to the created order. (Look back at week 1 to refresh your memory on the important role the created order plays in Scripture.) Paul's appeal to the created order demonstrates that he was not only referring to the women in Ephesus but to all women for all time. In a sense, Paul is saying that women, in the public assembly, are not to teach or exercise authority over men because God has put man in the role of spiritual leader of the church.[68]

From what we have studied, what is the significance of God not permitting a woman to teach a man?

Why do think women struggle with this command?

Teaching Authority Recap

I have given you a lot of information regarding 1 Timothy 2:9–15. Sometimes I find it's easier to grasp a difficult concept if you give me a bulleted version of the points. So here's what we studied regarding the teaching authority of the church. Why does God not allow women to teach men when we gather for worship?

- **Teaching holds greater authority than other spiritual gifts** (James 3:1). We have already discussed the primary importance of teaching in the New Testament. Teaching doctrine was above prophecy, evangelism, and other forms of public speaking. Therefore, when the church gathered together in the public assembly, men should take the lead in teaching.[69]
- **Teaching authority is based on the created order, which places men as the spiritual leader of the home and the church.** When the assembly gathers for worship and teaching, both men and women are present, including the elders of the church. Paul appeals to the created order to show that men—not women—are to be the spiritual leaders. Therefore, when the assembly

gathers, the women are not to take authority over the men because they would be undermining the teaching authority of the elder.[70]

- **A woman is to learn with a teachable and quiet spirit.** In 1 Timothy 2:11–12, Paul uses the phrases "learn in silence" and "be silent." In both verses, he uses the same Greek word for "quiet," which doesn't mean complete silence or keeping your mouth shut. Instead, he encourages women to learn and study Scripture, but do so with a teachable attitude.

The command to not "teach or exercise authority over a man" is consistent with the rest of Scripture. In verses 13–15, Paul appeals to the created order that Adam was the one created first. God has always had man as the spiritual head of the family and the physical church. Men are capable of learning from women, and Paul does not forbid a woman to never teach a man.[71] But, when the church assembly gathered together, then the women were to learn in an attitude of submission with a teachable spirit.

ℰℭ

If you have the gift of teaching, then teach. We need women to step up and teach women's Sunday school classes and become teachers and mentors to youth/college girls. Ladies, we have an important job to do. Let's get busy doing it.

ℰℭ

How would you explain 1 Timothy 2:9–15 to a friend?

What objections do you have or have you heard about women not teaching men?

Good work today, ladies! Thank you for hanging in there. My prayer is that you are beginning to see a God who has opened the door for us to have a fulfilling ministry instead of a God who only limits us. We spend so much time focusing on what we *"can't" do* that we lose sight of what God is calling us *to do*. If you have the gift of teaching, then teach. We need women to step up and teach women's Sunday school classes and become teachers and mentors to youth/college girls. Ladies, we have an important job to do. Let's get busy doing it.

HEAD COVERINGS: A PECULIAR PRACTICE

We have come to the last passage in our discussion. (I heard that sigh of relief.) Do you realize that you just spent a week taking a mini seminary course? You have worked hard, studied well, and I see God doing a mighty work in your heart. Don't give up. We have one more passage to discuss, and you'll be happy to know that it doesn't involve us being quiet. (Praise the Lord, because I'm a bit of a loud mouth.)

Today, we turn our attention to a peculiar practice: the wearing of a head covering. I've worn a baseball cap or visor to exercise, but I've never worn a head covering in church. So, are women required to wear a head covering when they pray? If not, what message does this passage have for Christian women? These are just two of a few questions we will study to gain clarity. Before you begin this session, pray and ask God to open your heart and mind to the truth of His Word. After you've prayed, begin.

Read 1 Corinthians 11:2–16. I want you to use the hermeneutical guidelines and see if you can draw some conclusions on your own. You can do it!

What is clear in this passage?

What is confusing in this passage?

Based on what we have already discussed about headship and authority, how would you interpret this passage?

Context Matters

We've already looked at the Corinthian church in the passage dealing with women remaining silent in the church. In today's passage, Paul is addressing the same group of people and answering the same questions they wrote to him. Remember, we only have the answers to the Corinthians' questions; we don't have the questions themselves.

In chapter 8, Paul addresses foods sacrificed to idols. Corinth was known for its immoral lifestyle, and the main religion was the worship of Aphrodite, the goddess of love. Therefore, the church of Corinth obviously asked Paul how to respond to eating foods that were sacrificed to idols. Paul told the Corinthian Christians that it was not sinful to eat foods sacrificed to idols because idols are not real gods—there is only one God, which is the living God (v. 4). However, he does tell them—if they choose to eat food sacrificed to idols—to make sure they don't cause a weaker brother or sister in Christ to stumble. Therefore, if they had a weaker sister who thought it was sinful to eat food sacrificed to idols, then they should be willing to refrain from eating.

In chapter 9, Paul explains his rights as an apostle of Christ. He tells them he is free to do many things like taking a wife who is a Christian (v. 5), eating and drinking what he wants (v. 4), and being paid for his work in the gospel ministry (vv. 13–14). But Paul does not exercise his rights because he is more concerned with people coming to faith in Christ than he is his own rights. The key verse of this chapter is: "To the weak I became weak, in order to win the weak. I have become all things to all people, so that I may by every possible means save some" (1 Cor. 9:22). In saying this, Paul sets forth an example of humility for the church of Corinth—and us—to follow.

In chapter 10, Paul returns to talking about idolatry. He confronts their tendency to indulge in sexual immorality, and he explains to them the judgment that will come upon them if they continue in their sin. Paul also addresses the misconception that sin is too powerful for a Christian to overcome. He reminds the Corinthians that God will provide for them an escape in the moment of temptation, but they must be willing to not give in and indulge the flesh (vv. 12–13).

We have finally come to our focal passage. In chapter 11, Paul addresses the use of head coverings and the Lord's Supper. He turns from instructing them individually to giving them instructions for when they gather as a body of believers. He continues his instructions for the public assembly in chapters

12–14. Paul concludes his letter by affirming the bodily resurrection of Christ and what that truth means for Christians.

What most spoke to you about the context?

What seems to be the theme of the context?

To Wear or Not to Wear Head Coverings? That is the Question

"To wear or not to wear head coverings" is the central question we want to answer. There are some Christian denominations, such as the Mennonites, who wear a head covering. However, most evangelical churches have ceased this practice. Are we correct or allowed to not adhere to this command, or should we go back to wearing head coverings in worship services? In order to understand Paul's meaning and use of a head covering, we must look at the hermeneutical guidelines laid out for us at the beginning of the week.

What is clear in this passage?

There are a few things that are clear in 1 Corinthians 11:2–16. In verse 3, Paul appeals to headship. He says, "But I want you to know that Christ is the head of every man, and the man is the head of the woman, and God is the head of Christ." Though there is some confusion with this verse, especially in regards to the equal yet functional roles of the

Trinity, God is very clear about headship and proper authority. Secondly, Paul gives permission for both men and women to pray and prophesy in the assembly (vv. 4–5). We have studied at length the difference between women teaching men and women praying and prophesying in the assembly, so we will not discuss it in this section. And finally, Paul tells the Corinthians to stop making a mockery of the Lord's Supper (vv. 20–22). He warns them against getting drunk and overeating during communion. Instead, communion should first be taken after a time of reflection, repentance, and forgiveness (vv. 28–29). He ends the chapter telling them that he will address their other questions when he comes to see them (v. 34).

Do you see any other clear teaching in 1 Corinthians 11? If so, write it here.

What is confusing in this passage?

I admit, 1 Corinthians 11:2–16 is definitely full of more confusing statements than clear statements. However, we will consider two particular verses to help us get to the interpretation of this passage—1 Corinthians 11:3 and 5. Let's first address 1 Corinthians 11:5. It says, "But every woman who prays or prophesies with her head uncovered dishonors her head, since that is one and the same as having her head shaved." Is Paul suggesting that Christian women put on a veil in order to show their submission to their husband? To understand, the meaning of head covering and its application for today, we first need to consider what a head covering symbolized in Corinth.

New Testament Meaning of Head Covering

Head coverings in the New Testament had a different meaning than they do today. There are three possible considerations for a head covering in the New Testament.

- **A head covering was not a full veil but more of a shawl.** According to one scholar, a head covering was not the full veil that is worn by Muslims, but a shawl that wrapped around a woman's shoulders. We get this understanding because of Paul's usage of the Greek word *peribolaion* (pronounced per-ib-ol'-ah-yon), which is translated "covering" in verse 15. *Peribolaion* refers to a shawl of some sort and not a full veil.[72]
- **A head covering distinguished women from men.** Have you ever watched *Passion of the Christ* or *Jesus of Nazareth*? If so, then you probably noticed both the men and women wearing long robes and sandals. Since their clothing was basically identical, a woman's long hair and head covering set women apart from men.[73] The full head covering was an adornment that was reserved only for women.
- **A head covering was a symbol of a married woman's submission to her husband.** A woman who did not wear a head covering but instead wore her hair loose around her shoulders was considered insubordinate or mimicking a prostitute. (Prostitutes and wild women wore their long hair undone.)[74] Therefore, when a woman wore a head covering, she was showing her society that (1) she was married and (2) she respected her husband.

Though the explanations of the meaning of head coverings vary among scholars, there is one consistent message. There is a proper way for a woman to dress and conduct herself.

Ladies, we are not to dress like men, and men are not to dress like women. Also, we, as Christian women, should respect and esteem our husbands in private and especially in public.

The Meaning of the Word *Kephalē*

Another confusing aspect of this passage is Paul's meaning and use of the word *kephalē*, which is translated "head." (Get your thinking caps on; we are about to dive headlong into the original language. Hang in there and see what God will teach you.) First Corinthians 11:3 says, "But I want you to know that Christ is the head of every man, and the man is the head of the woman, and God is the head of Christ."

What word do you see repeated three times?

It doesn't take a Bible scholar to realize the purpose of 1 Corinthians 11:3 is to point out the importance of headship and submission. However, egalitarians ask, If Jesus is fully God, then how can He be submissive to Himself? Their argument goes like this: If Jesus is submissive to God, then Jesus ceases to be God. Therefore, evangelical feminists change the traditional meaning of *kephalē* from "head" to "source." Gordon Fee states, "According to 1 Corinthians 8:6, all things (including Adam) were created 'through Christ'; the man then became the 'source' of the woman's being, while God was the 'source' of Christ's incarnation."[75]

In using "source" as a metaphor for "head," egalitarians can remove the teaching of this passage: Just as man is to submit to Christ, a wife is to submit to her husband. Jesus, being both God and man, showed us the importance of authority and submission by submitting to the will of the Father (John

8:28–29; 14:28). As we learned in week 1, a difference in function or roles doesn't mean that there is a difference in essence or equality. Just because Jesus submitted to the will of the Father does not make Him any less God. And just because a wife submits to her husband's leadership doesn't mean she is inferior to man.[76]

I can hear some of you asking, Why is the meaning of "head" important to this passage? Well, I'm glad you asked. The theme, which leads to the interpretation of 1

&)CR

The theme, which leads to the interpretation of 1 Corinthians 11:2–16, is authority and submission. If you remove authority and submission from the passage, then the passage does not make much sense. It then becomes an unclear passage on the clothing attire of the women in Corinth.

&)CR

Corinthians 11:2–16, is authority and submission. If you remove authority and submission from the passage, then the passage does not make much sense. It then becomes an unclear passage on the clothing attire of the women in Corinth.

In understanding 1 Corinthians 11:2–16, we must remember that before Paul even mentions the usage of head coverings, he first appeals to authority and submission (v. 3). Paul then explains to the church of Corinth how the men and women are to show their submission to Christ and specifically how women are to show their submission to their husbands (vv. 4–10). Therefore, we can interpret 1 Corinthians 11:2–16 as meaning: In order to show their submission to Christ and their husbands, the women should wear a head covering when they pray and prophesy.

How would you explain 1 Corinthians 11:2–16 to a friend?

Why is the meaning of "head" so important to this passage?

How does this interpretation fit with the rest of Scripture?

If we assume the theme of the passage is authority and submission and the usage of a head covering symbolized a woman's submission to her husband, then this teaching—a woman should cover her head when she prays and prophesies— is consistent with Scripture. We have discussed in depth the importance of a Christian woman being submissive, first to Christ and then to her husband. Paul again emphasizes submission by appealing to Jesus' example of submission to God (v. 3) and then appealing to the created order (vv. 8–9).

How does the use of a head covering apply to us?

We still have not answered the question of the use or lack of use of head coverings for today. Are Christian women to wear a head covering in the modern church? To answer that question, let's review the meaning of a head covering in the New Testament.

- **A head covering set women apart from men.** A head covering and long hair signified that a woman was indeed a woman. A man was not to wear a head covering because it would mean he was adorning himself as a woman, which would be shameful (v. 4). (Using an example from modern society, it would be like a man wearing a dress.)[77]

- **A head covering showed that a woman was married.** In Corinth, it appears that an unmarried woman did not wear a head covering. So, the head covering set apart the married women from the unmarried women.[78]

- **The head covering was a symbol of a woman's submission to her husband.** Therefore, when women gathered in the public assembly, they were to adorn themselves with a head covering when they prophesied and prayed. In doing so, they symbolized to the men and women present that they were indeed under God's authority and living in submission to their husband's authority.[79]

We have *finally* come to the main question regarding this passage:

 REST STOP: In American evangelical churches, are head coverings a symbol of a woman's submission to her husband?

In most evangelical churches, the use of a head covering does *not* symbolize to the unbelieving world that a woman is under the authority of her husband. Certainly, it is not wrong or inappropriate for a married woman to wear a hat or some sort of head covering in church, but it is not a necessary custom in America. I like Wayne Grudem's response to this question. He encourages married women to wear whatever symbolizes, in their culture, that a woman is married.[80]

In America, what is the symbol a woman wears to show she is married?

If you answered: "she wears a wedding ring," then you are correct! In American culture, married women wear a ring on their left hand. However, in other cultures it is something different. I have a friend who lives in an East Asian country. The married women wear different colored clothing than unmarried women. Therefore, in that culture it would be fitting for a Christian woman to wear the appropriate color that symbolized she is a married woman.

Ladies, there is much freedom that comes with being a follower of Christ. In Paul's letters to the Corinthians, he addresses many of those freedoms and encourages new believers to walk in that freedom. But, women are not free to disrespect their husbands. Paul also shows that headship is a command that should not be overlooked. Christian married women are still called to obey this passage, which is to show that they are under the authority of their husbands.

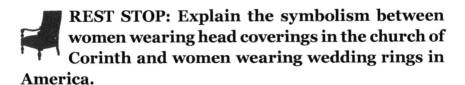 **REST STOP: Explain the symbolism between women wearing head coverings in the church of Corinth and women wearing wedding rings in America.**

How would you defend someone who accuses you of obeying one passage but not the other? (Example: You believe that women shouldn't teach men, but you don't wear a head covering.)

Ladies, good work today! I am proud of you for sticking with me this week and working through each of these passages. My prayer is that you gained insight on how to interpret difficult passages that seem to be impossible. Anytime you come across a difficult passage, go back to the hermeneutical guidelines, and then systematically work through it. You have the tools necessary to do it and the Holy Spirit giving you insight. Please don't shy away from them. I also pray you realized that every part of Scripture can teach us something. God doesn't hide His Word from us. Instead, He wants us to come to Him with a humble spirit and seek to pull out the truths that are present.

Week 6

THE DESTINATION:
WOMEN CELEBRATED IN MINISTRY

Can you believe this is our last week together? We've traveled many spiritual miles and covered a lot of territory these last five weeks. I'm so proud of you. We've laughed, told stories, struggled, and hopefully grown in our identity as a woman. Ladies, my prayer, more than anything, is that you've seen God's heart toward you. He loves you, and He considers you valuable to His kingdom. He put you here—whether single, married with children, married without children, or widowed—to be involved in teaching and discipling the next generation of leaders. Let's be faithful to the task.

We will finish our journey looking at the women in Jesus' and Paul's ministries. Complementarians are often accused of limiting women in ministry and treating women as second-class ministers instead of coheirs with Christ. This week I hope to demolish that myth. Jesus and Paul—yes Paul—had women who served as influencers alongside them and were instrumental in their ministries. I want us to look at some of these women and see how God used them and their gifts in His kingdom's work. God has so much for us to do, and I want us to know what it is, and then get busy doing it.

JEWISH WOMEN IN THE FIRST CENTURY

We've already looked at how the Pharisees viewed women—which wasn't good—but I want us to look a little closer at the protection Jewish women had in the first century. To be honest with you, these women weren't given the level of respect we know in the twenty-first century, but they were given more respect than women in other cultures. For example, though Roman girls were allowed to have a basic education, the Romans considered women property and treated them like slaves. However, Jewish women weren't considered property and were deemed worthy of honor (Prov. 31). Whenever Jewish girls got married, their fathers were given a bride price. The purpose of it was twofold—first, to help with the loss of her as a worker in the father's home, and second, to be used by her if she divorced or was sent away without just cause.[81]

Jewish rabbis were often accused of neglecting and belittling women, however, the Jewish culture gave more value and dignity to women than was deemed appropriate for their time period.[82] For example, under the Law of Moses, both women and men were held responsible for adultery. A man bore the responsibility for bringing an accused wife before the priests to determine her guilt or innocence, and he could not stone her or divorce her without due process (Num. 5:11–31). Jewish slave women were also protected, which wasn't common in the first century. If a woman was captured in war, the man was commanded to allow her to mourn her parents for a month, and then he was to marry her. If she failed to bring him delight, he was not permitted to sell her to another man or abuse her. Instead, he was commanded to let her go freely (Deut. 21:10–14).[83]

Women were also protected in divorce proceedings. In Matthew 5:31–32, Jesus gives a more severe warning for men who choose to divorce their wives. He says that if a man divorces his wife for reasons besides adultery, then he forces her to commit adultery. This command, first, shows the importance of the marriage relationship, and secondly, it shows the value that Jesus had for women. A husband could not merely send his wife away, which meant she lost all status and protection in society. Instead, the husband was commanded to stay with her and protect her.

These are just a few of the examples in which Jews were different from neighboring societies. In Genesis 1–2, God created men and women equal. And, He has the same love for women as He does for men. Therefore, it is natural that God would use us—His special creation—to further His kingdom's agenda.

In reading the Old Testament, have you ever become frustrated—even angered—at laws regarding women in Exodus to Deuteronomy? Does this short history lesson change some of your preconceived ideas of the treatment of women? Explain.

Ladies, this week is full of great spiritual and practical applications for us in ministry. Therefore, before you begin each section I want you to read the verses or passage related to each woman. I will give you a shortened version of her story, but you will want the richness of what is found in the written text. After you read, we will take a closer look at each woman's story. Let's get started!

WOMEN WHO FOUND JESUS

The Woman with a Blood Issue

We don't know the name of this woman, but her story is recorded in three of the four Gospels (Matt. 9:20–22; Mark 5:25–34; Luke 8:43–48). Under the Jewish law, if a woman had a discharge of blood that lasted longer than her menstrual cycle, she was considered unclean until the bleeding or discharge ceased (Lev. 15:25). This meant she was not allowed to worship at the temple, be in relationship with people, and anyone who touched her would be considered unclean. Basically, this woman was an outcast and in desperate need of healing.

The gospel of Mark gives us some interesting details of her life. In Mark 5:25, the gospel writer said she had been hemorrhaging for twelve years and had "suffered much" under the care of the doctors. (Can you imagine going twelve years without a handshake, hug, or simple pat on the back? This woman was dying inside.) However, instead of getting better, this woman was getting worse. Needless to say, she had come to the end of her rope, and she knew Jesus was her only hope for healing. Therefore, she broke Jewish custom and reached out to touch just the hem of Jesus' robe. Immediately, Jesus felt power come out of Him, and He began to inquire as to who touched Him (Mark 5:30). Trembling and with much fear, the woman came to Him and confessed that she was the one who touched Him. Jesus looked at her (I can just see the compassion and love in His eyes) and called her "Daughter," which indicated His deep respect for her. From that moment, this woman found healing and was restored back to complete health. She could now worship with the rest of the women, and her place in society was restored.

What can we learn from Jesus' encounter with this woman?

Jesus was not afraid to go against social customs and ritual uncleanness laws in order to restore a woman to physical and spiritual health. Since the woman touched Him, Jesus was considered unclean in the eyes of the Jewish priests. Instead of rebuking her and demoralizing her in front of the crowd, Jesus looked on her with love and compassion—and then healed her. Since she was no longer considered unclean, she could go to the temple and offer her sacrifices.[84] Jesus cared about this woman and offered her what doctors could not offer, healing and restoration. And He can and will do the same for you.

REST STOP: Do you need a healing—whether spiritual or physical—touch from Jesus today? If so, write a prayer expressing that to Him. He is faithful and wants to bring healing to our lives.

The Sinful Woman Who Washed Jesus' Feet

Once again, we aren't given this woman's name. However, Luke 7:36–50 records her story. This encounter occurs during the week of Passover. Jesus was soon to be executed on a Roman cross, where He would be the sin atonement for humanity. On this particular day, Jesus was with His disciples at Simon's (a Pharisee) house. All of a sudden, an unnamed woman came in weeping, began to pour a costly ointment on His feet, and then wiped her tears from his feet with her hair. Immediately, the disciples and Simon were amazed and appalled at Jesus allowing this sinful woman to touch Him. The disciples were angry and rebuked her because she was wasting the perfume when it could be sold to give money to the poor. (I can just see their sneers and haughty looks.) Jesus, knowing the thoughts and heart intentions of the guests, decided to use this incident as a teachable moment.

Jesus, and the rest of the men present, knew the great sin of this woman. However, whenever Jesus looked at this woman, He saw a sinful, desperate woman who was in need of forgiveness. Therefore, Jesus rebuked Simon for not using the customary greetings of his day (no water for His feet, no kiss of greeting, and no anointing of His head with oil), and then Jesus commended the woman for her faith. He forgave her sin and sent her on her way.

What can we learn from Jesus' encounter with this sinful woan?

Jesus was willing to associate with all sinners, both great and small. In Luke 7:39, Simon reasoned in his heart that Jesus must not be a prophet because He allowed a woman—a sinner—to touch Him. Yet, Jesus unashamedly forgave and restored the woman.

ಬು ಆ

Ladies, if you are caught up in a cycle of sin, know that Jesus is not intimidated or ashamed of you. He offers love, grace, and forgiveness to you. Would you be willing to repent of your sin and turn back to Him?

ಬು ಆ

Ladies, if you are caught up in a cycle of sin, know that Jesus is not intimidated or ashamed of you. He offers love, grace, and forgiveness to you. Would you be willing to repent of your sin and turn back to Him? I am so glad that Jesus taught that we, regardless of our sinful past, are offered forgiveness and welcomed into His kingdom.

Have you been running from God because of a sinful past or present? Stop right now, turn around (repent), seek His forgiveness, and let Him restore you. If this is your heart's desire, express that to Him.

The Samaritan Woman

This portion of Scripture reads like a good story. You know how a story gets even better when you know the background of it? Well, let me share with you what was really going on in John 4 and the ways that Jesus could have responded to the Samaritan woman.

John 4:4 says that Jesus "had to travel through Samaria." Jews and Samaritans didn't like each other, and Jews took great caution to not go through Samaria. So, when you read that Jesus "had to travel through," it doesn't mean that Jesus went through Samaria because there was no alternative route. The word "had"—in the Greek—literally means that something (the Holy Spirit) compelled Him to go through Samaria.[85] Jesus was obligated by a sense of responsibility to go through Samaria. Jesus, being fully God, knew there would be a woman sitting at that well who needed Him.

Jesus comes to Samaria and encounters a woman. She came to draw water from the well of Jacob, and the text says it is noon (sixth hour). Most women came to the well in the morning, but here she was at the hottest part of the day. Why? More than likely, she was a social outcast and didn't want to deal with the haughty looks and snickering at the hands of the town's women. Everyone in town knew this woman's reputation—she had been married five times, and the man she lived with was not her husband. (If you have in mind the town harlot, then you're right on track.) I can just imagine the look of shock that was on her face when Jesus, a Jew, spoke to her. In fact, John 4:9 records her confusion. But, Jesus had a greater purpose than just breaking Jewish custom when He spoke to the Samaritan woman.

John 4:10–26 records Jesus' conversation with this outcast woman. Jesus asks her for water, which opened the door for Him to tell her about the "living water" only He can give. (Ladies, Jesus is always more concerned with meeting our spiritual needs first.) He then tells her that she had been married five times, and the man she currently lives with is not her husband. A woman with five previous husbands is a little much in our day (hello, Elizabeth Taylor), but it would have been unimaginable in her day.[86] After recovering from a stranger's familiarity with her life, she realized that Jesus was more than just a man … He was the Messiah, the One she had been waiting to come and offer her salvation. Immediately, the woman ran off proclaiming to her town that the Messiah had come, and she had been changed.

What can we learn from Jesus' encounter with the Samaritan woman?

Jesus was not ashamed to minister to a woman tainted by sin. Most men would have either looked on her with disgust or turned the other way. Instead, Jesus spoke words of healing and life over her. Secondly, you see in John 4:39 that many Samaritans believed in Jesus *because* of this woman's testimony of Him. Jesus used her to bring the gospel message to the Samaritans—a half-breed of Jews and Gentiles—showing that salvation was open to all people. She isn't your typical evangelist, but she knew and experienced the forgiveness and freedom that only Jesus could give. This woman's newfound freedom made her share her story with whoever would listen.

REST STOP: What is your story? You may not be the town harlot, but we have all been forgiven of something. Do you share your story of forgiveness to whoever will listen? If not, what is stopping you?

WOMEN WHO FOLLOWED JESUS

Mary, Jesus' Mother (Luke 1:26–56; John 2:1–12; Acts 1:14)

Scripture is careful to share bits and pieces of Mary's life with us. Probably the most famous passage is in Luke 1–2—the Christmas story. In Luke 1, Luke records the account of the angel, Gabriel, coming to Mary as he hails her as the "favored" one (Luke 1:28). God saw in this teenage girl someone who was humble, giving, and capable of being the mother of the Savior. She was not perfect, but she was willing to do whatever God asked of her. I can only imagine the ridicule she received when it was known she was pregnant, and Joseph was not the father. (To be honest with you—if she had been one of my girls—I don't think I would have believed her either. Such a strange story!) In fact, Matthew 13:54–58, gives us a glimpse into Nazareth's perception of Jesus. Matthew says that they "took offense" at Him and refused to believe in Him as Messiah. This proves that God will sometimes ask us to do unpopular things, and the world will not understand.

Has God ever asked you to do something you didn't understand and your parents or friends definitely didn't understand?

How did you respond when you were ridiculed? Were you obedient, or did you run from the assignment?

Mary followed Jesus throughout His earthly ministry. Scripture gives us snapshots of Mary supporting Jesus (Luke 8:19–21), ministering to Jesus (Matt. 27:55–56), anointing Jesus' body for burial (Luke 23:55–56), and later worshipping at the risen Savior's feet and then proclaiming His resurrection to the disciples (Matt. 28:8–10). Mary went from caring for Jesus as an infant and child to being one of His followers. She knew the uniqueness of her Son's life, and she was willing to follow Him wherever He went. The last time Scriptures mentions Mary is in Acts 1:14. We see Mary with the other disciples waiting for the promised Holy Spirit. She had been with Him from conception to ascension, and she believed in Him. There is no doubt that she proclaimed Jesus' Messiahship until her last days.

Mary possibly knew Jesus better than any other person, yet she followed Him. What do you think that says of her character and Jesus' character?

What can we learn from Jesus' relationship with Mary?

Mary was a faithful follower. First, we see Mary as a normal, humble woman who God used in mighty ways. She was not divine, and she did not remain an eternal virgin (Matt. 13:55–56). Jesus was also very careful to not elevate her above other women and acknowledged her as a fallen human in need of a savior (John 2:1–12; Luke 11:27–28). Secondly, we see that Jesus respected Mary and cared for her. While He was dying on the cross, He, as her firstborn son, made sure that she would be cared for after His ascension. He made provisions for her and asked John to take her into his home as his mother (John 19:26–27). Jesus knew His place as Messiah, yet He respected and honored His mother and cared for her needs.

Finally, Mary is an example of someone who followed Jesus to the end (Acts 1:14). Acts 1:14 is the last place we see Mary in Scripture.

What is Mary doing in Acts 1:14?

She was waiting—along with 120 others—for God's Holy Spirit. In a few moments, both men and women were going to receive the Holy Spirit. His coming would give them boldness and power to take the gospel message to the ends of the earth. Though we don't get to see any more of Mary's life, we can be assured that she was faithful to tell of her son's life, ministry, death, and resurrection to anyone who was willing to listen. She was faithful to the end.

Read 2 Timothy 4:6–8. Are you allowing your life to be poured out for the gospel of Christ? What needs to change in your life (a friendship, career, significant relationship) in order to finish well and be faithful to the end?

Martha and Mary of Bethany (Luke 10:38–42; John 11:1–44; John 12:1–8)

Mary and Martha were sisters who were friends of Jesus. One of the most familiar stories of these sisters is in Luke 10:38–42. Luke tells of Mary sitting at Jesus' feet while Martha was busy serving. When this passage is taught, Martha is often chastised for her serving, but most women can empathize with her plight. She invites an important guest into her home, and her sister does nothing to help. How many of us are guilty for putting service above sitting? (I know I am.)

This passage teaches women two great truths. First, women tend to become distracted in serving and miss sitting at Jesus' feet and developing a relationship with Him. As women, we need to stop our busyness and learn to sit at Jesus' feet and learn from Him. Secondly, this passage shows that Jesus wanted women to learn from Him. In that day, it was not customary for a woman to learn from a rabbi, but Jesus specifically commended Mary for her desire to learn.

Do you tend to be more of a Martha or a Mary? Explain your answer.

Let's try to be both—women who serve *and* women who sit.

What can we learn from Jesus' relationship with Mary and Martha?

There are two key lessons we can learn from Jesus' friendship with Mary and Martha. First, Jesus asks us to come, sit at His feet, and learn from Him. Christianity is not just for men—Praise the Lord! We need more women who are willing to learn the great mysteries of Christ and then share that with a lost world. We need women to step up and be willing to learn and to teach others. Jesus commended Mary for her interest in learning from Him and then encouraged Martha to do the same.

Secondly, Jesus allowed women into His inner circle of friends. Though Jesus picked twelve men to be in His inner circle of disciples, He still made room for women to serve with Him. He welcomed them to learn from Him, and He did not keep them from becoming His friends. Jesus showed respect for women and rebuked men who did not show them the same respect and honor (John 12:7–8).

Mary Magdalene (Luke 8:1–3; 23:55—24;12 Matt. 27:55–61; 28:1–10)

Mary Magdalene went from Jesus finding her to following Him. In Luke 8:1–3, Scripture says that Jesus cast out seven demons from her. Imagine the relief, joy, and freedom she felt after being set free from the torment of demons! After her deliverance, she began to follow Jesus. Scripture does not say what Mary did for a living or how she acquired her financial resources, but she obviously had enough money to provide financial assistance for Jesus' earthly ministry. Numerous times in Scripture, there is a reference of her following Jesus and providing financially for Him. Scripture doesn't say she is married, but one can assume she was not married because there is no mention of a husband. Regardless of her marital status, Jesus showed deep gratitude for her as she served Him through financial means.

Mary was also the one to whom Jesus first appeared in His resurrected body. John 20:11–18 records Jesus appearing to Mary after His resurrection. She, along with several other women, went to the tomb to anoint Jesus' body with spices. When they discovered the stone was rolled away and the tomb was empty, they assumed His body had been taken. Mary stayed at the tomb weeping, and Jesus appeared to her. After revealing Himself to her, Jesus gave Mary the command to go and tell His disciples of His resurrection.

What can we learn from Jesus' relationship with Mary Magdalene?

First, there is a ministry Jesus has called every woman to do—and that includes you. Mary provided for Jesus' financial needs, and she was one of the first evangelists.

Okay ... time out. Before we go further with celebrating the giftedness of women, I want to clear up a few misconceptions about women's roles. Because of women's service to Him and for Him, egalitarians claim

There is a ministry Jesus has called every woman to do—and that includes you.

that Jesus called Mary and other women apostles—which is not supported by Scripture. This is the rationale: Since Jesus allowed women to serve Him, minister alongside Him, and proclaim His resurrection, it shows that He abolished all roles of men and women and opened the possibility of women holding all positions in church leadership, specifically the teaching ministry over men.[87] However, Mary's financial giving is not an apostleship role but a supporting role. And, Mary's proclamation of Jesus' resurrection is not a teaching role but an evangelistic role. Christians—both men and women—are called to give to and to proclaim the gospel message. Ladies,

Jesus doesn't call us to disregard our God-ordained roles, but He does invite us to learn from Him and proclaim His gospel message to anyone who will listen. Okay … time in.

Secondly, Jesus taught that a woman's word is to be valued. In the first century, a woman was not considered a reliable witness. (In fact, you had to have two or three witnesses to verify what a woman said.) This is evident in the fact that the disciples did not believe her when she announced Jesus' resurrection (Luke 24:11). However, Jesus strategically appeared to the women first, and then gave them the privilege of being the first to proclaim His resurrection.[88]

Do you actively share your faith with others, or do you hide your relationship with Jesus?

REST STOP: Would you be willing to recommit or commit for the first time to share what Jesus has done in your life? If so, write that as a prayer below.

Out of the six women in Jesus' ministry, whose story resonated most with your heart? Why?

Ladies, Jesus calls us to be actively involved in ministry. Christianity is not a relationship and ministry reserved only for men, but Jesus commands for both men and women to proclaim Him as Lord and tell a lost world about His death and resurrection.

WOMEN IN PAUL'S MINISTRY

Women are also part of the ministry God gave Paul. Paul has received a lot of negative attention for his teaching on women in ministry. He has been accused of being a sexist, male chauvinist pig who sought to belittle women in their desire to worship and serve God. But, was Paul really antiwomen, or did he see a place for women in ministry? Let's find out.

Lydia (Acts 16:11-15, 40)

I love Lydia's story. There's something about her that I connect with. In Acts 16:6–10, God gives Paul a burden (or calling) to go to Macedonia. One evening, Paul had a vision of a man calling him to come and help him. So, they went. Scripture says that Paul, Timothy, Silas, and Luke were in Philippi (a city in Macedonia) several days before the Sabbath. On the Sabbath they went out of the city to the place that is known for prayer. There were women present, and the men began to talk to them. One woman, Lydia, "a worshipper of God," believed what Paul was saying about Jesus, and she put her faith in Christ. Lydia became the first convert in the European continent. I find it fascinating, and even humorous, that the "man" calling Paul to Macedonia to help him turned out to be a woman.[89]

Lydia was probably a wealthy woman due to her business. She made and sold purple cloth, which was an expensive cloth sold mainly to royalty and the wealthy.[90] Her wealth allowed her a large enough home to house Paul and his associates.

Scripture actually says that Lydia tested the men. She said they could prove to her they believed the validity of her conversion by staying at her house. She was persistent in hospitality. Eventually, a church began in Philippi, and Paul wrote to them about the joy they brought to him because of their faith (Phil. 1:3–11). (Before moving on, go back and read Acts 16. Lydia's story is amazing.)

Are you willing to allow your home to be used for ministry? If not, what's stopping you? If so, share a story of how you've been blessed by people you've hosted.

What does Lydia's example show us about women in ministy?

Lydia's conversion to Christ indicates Paul valued women and their eternal salvation. This Scripture passage doesn't mention men present at the place of prayer. However, Paul and his associates didn't shy away from engaging in spiritual conversations with them. Secondly, Lydia was a businesswoman. As we have learned, Scripture teaches that the primary job a woman is called to do is to care for her home. But, Scripture also shows examples of women who owned their own businesses and used that money for ministry. Ladies, there isn't a one-size-fits-all model for ministry. God uses all of us in

Ladies, there isn't a one-size-fits-all model for ministry. God uses all of us in very different ways to accomplish the same goal— the spread of the gospel.

very different ways to accomplish the same goal—the spread of the gospel.

Lastly, God used Lydia's home as the beginning place for the spread of the gospel on the European continent.[91] Some egalitarians teach that Lydia's conversion and use of her home to begin the church in Europe shows that Jesus' death and resurrection obliterated any gender roles for the New Testament church.[92] Yet, if you read Acts 16, there is no mention of Lydia having a teaching or leading role over the men or the church that met in her house. Instead, Scripture focuses solely on her hospitality to Paul and his associates. Lydia continued to be an influence in the church of Philippi (yes an influence), and she is remembered for her contribution to Paul's ministry.

How can you use your resources—home, money, talents—to minister to those in need?

Phoebe (Rom. 16:1-2)

There are only two verses of Scripture that speak of a woman named Phoebe, but her name and function in the church has caused quite the theological wave. In Romans 16:1–2, Paul commends Phoebe for three specific things. First was her service *to* the church in Cenchreae—which is a port in Corinth. Most scholars agree that Phoebe was probably the person who carried Paul's letter to the Roman church. This act showed Paul's great respect and trust in her as a partner in the gospel ministry.[93]

Paul also commended her for being a "servant *of* the church." The term "servant" can also be translated "deaconess." In the first century, a deaconess aided widows, helped the sick, assisted in the baptism of women converts to Christianity, and facilitated in the teaching and discipling of women.[94] Some complementarian scholars note that she probably had some sort of responsibility in the Cenchreae church, but the type of responsibility is unknown. All that is said of her is that she aided Paul in his ministry and had a servant's heart.[95]

Lastly, Phoebe was commended for being a "patron of many" (Rom. 16:2 ESV). The word "patron" is also translated "help" or "benefactress," which meant that Phoebe was probably a wealthy woman. Undoubtedly, she gave financial assistance to Paul and other ministers of the gospel. She not only helped Paul in his ministry, but she helped others.[96]

Because of Phoebe's controversial role in Romans, I want us to look more at the evangelical feminist's view of her. Paul's mention of her in Romans has become a rallying cry for women as having the same roles as men in the early church. Though some evangelical feminists are more complementarian in their view of Phoebe by stating the term *diakonos* (deacon) is a general statement of someone who serves,[97] some egalitarians conclude that Phoebe had a more formal role—such as being an official, ranking representative to another church.[98] Egalitarians also assume that she, like Paul, had some sort of pastoral leadership and teaching authority within the church. Since the same word *diakonos* is used to describe both Paul and Phoebe, egalitarians teach that Phoebe stands as an example of a woman who preached the gospel of Christ in an official leadership role.[99] I will save the complementarian view for the next section. But—for now—I want you to answer these questions.

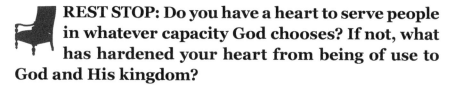

REST STOP: Do you have a heart to serve people in whatever capacity God chooses? If not, what has hardened your heart from being of use to God and His kingdom?

What does Phoebe's example show us about women in mnistry?

Paul had a deep respect for women, especially women who used their gifts to serve God and His kingdom. Paul is often accused of being sexist, but these verses show his great admiration for a woman who ministered *alongside him* for the gospel ministry. Phoebe also shows us the importance of women serving the local body of believers. A woman can offer assistance, even financial assistance, to the body and

ℰ ℭ

Women should not shy away from leadership within the body, and they should allow God to use their spiritual gifts to serve the body of Christ. But, let's be careful that we don't become so overly zealous in our ministry pursuit that we step outside the boundaries God has given us.

ℰ ℭ

serve in the church without being a pastor. Romans 16:1–2 gives *no* indication that Phoebe was a pastor/teacher in the Cenchreaen church, but it does say that she served the members within the church and assisted men like Paul. Women should not shy away from leadership within the body, and they should allow God to use their spiritual gifts to serve the body of Christ. But, let's be careful that we don't become so overly zealous in our ministry pursuit that we step outside the boundaries God has given us.

Finally, this passage shows the importance of assisting ministers of the gospel. Some of the greatest mission-minded people are women who have a desire for the gospel to be spread throughout the world. Organizations such as the Women's Missionary Union (WMU) were started to educate young men and women in the importance of mission work. They assist missionaries through prayer, monetary means, and actually being on mission with them. Some of you can testify to the amazing things God has done because of the dedication and vision that some women had to take the gospel to the ends of the earth. Because of their efforts, there is now a missionary in every country of the world. Ladies, we must look for opportunities to get involved in serving ministers of the gospel and then serve them well.

How can you be involved in serving your pastor—or other staff members—at your church?

Pray that God would strengthen, protect, and equip your pastors to be the men of God and ministers He has called them to be.

Priscilla and Aquila (Acts 18:1-3; Acts 18:18-28; Rom. 16:3-5)

Priscilla and Aquila were a couple Paul commended in Romans 16:3–5, but their story is recorded in other parts of Scripture. Aquila, a Jewish man from Pontus, and his wife, Priscilla, were a couple who had great influence in the early church (Acts 18:2). Paul met them in Corinth, and he worked with them making tents. He also stayed with them, which probably meant he stayed in their home and worked out of their house (Acts 18:3). Priscilla and Aquila also worked together to explain the gospel of Christ more fully to Apollos (Acts 18:26). Apollos was a young, intelligent man who knew about Jesus and was a very good speaker. But he only knew of John's baptism, which was a baptism of repentance. (This reference means that he probably didn't know about the Holy Spirit's coming at Pentecost, nor did he know about the gospel being opened to the Gentiles.) And finally, Priscilla and Aquila "risked their necks" for Paul, which is a reference to them helping save him, with potentially great harm to themselves (Rom. 16:4). If someone saved my life, then I would definitely have affection for them that I didn't have for others (Rom. 16:3). With the ministry Priscilla and Aquila did together, a debate has formed about whether or not this couple's example gives women permission to publically teach men and be pastors of a congregation. Let's look at how the debate formed and then see if we can gain clarity on it.

Does Priscilla and Aquila's example give women permission to teach men and be pastors? Complementarians agree with egalitarians that Priscilla taught Apollos, for the text says it plainly (Acts 18:26). However, evangelical feminists teach that because Priscilla's name is given first in Acts 18:26, then she was probably the primary teacher and held the most authority. Egalitarians also assume that Priscilla had an ongoing habit of teaching men, and since a church met in their home, she probably taught the church that met in their home.[100]

&) C&

Ladies, Priscilla and Aquila are a great example of how God can use a couple to do amazing kingdom work. Don't shy away from being a part of this work.

&) C&

Another egalitarian argument is that there is no such thing as authoritative and unauthoritative teaching in Scripture. Therefore, when Priscilla taught or explained to Apollos more of the gospel, then Paul gives women permission to teach men without any conditions attached.[101] However, there is one major problem with this dispute. Scripture cannot contradict itself. (Remember our hermeneutical guidelines?) First Timothy 2:11–12 states that women should not teach or have authority over men. So, what in the world was Priscilla doing teaching Apollos?

Complementarians have a different view on Priscilla's teaching of Apollos. Scripture is clear that God gives spiritual gifts to all His children and those gifts are not based upon one's gender (Rom. 12:6–8). The Bible does not say to what extent Priscilla taught Apollos. She could have been the primary teacher, but regardless of how much and to what degree she taught this young man, the Bible says very plainly that this teaching was in private. She did not teach or rebuke him publically, but she taught him, *with* her husband, and in their *own* home.[102] This is significant, because nowhere in Scripture do you see Priscilla undermining the leadership of her husband or the male leadership of the church. The Bible clearly teaches that when the whole church congregation is gathered for worship, then the primary teaching and governing of the body is to be left to the men (1 Tim. 2:11–12; 1 Cor. 14:33–35).[103] God does give the gift of teaching to women, but He makes it clear that women are to primarily use their gifts to teach women and not publically exercise authority over men (Titus 2:2–5).

My husband and I understand this principle. Since Chris is a university pastor, we have countless opportunities to minister to young people. On occasion, a guy will ask to meet with both of us about an issue—normally it involves a girl. During our conversation, there is usually a point where Chris will turn to me and ask me to explain a question. There are certain topics, including biblical topics, where I have more training, and I can respond more accurately. Does that mean that I undermine my husband's leadership? No! In fact, I respond to his leadership by answering the question. Does the young man gain biblical understanding from my counsel? I pray he does.

Ladies, Priscilla and Aquila are a great example of how God can use a couple to do amazing kingdom work. Don't shy away from being a part of this work.

What does Priscilla and Aquila's example show us about women in ministry?

There are two main lessons we can learn from Priscilla's example. First, women should not shy away from the teaching ministry. Ladies, the church needs more women to passionately study God's Word, become equipped to teach the Word, and then get out there and teach. Priscilla knew enough about Scripture to correct someone who was not fully teaching the gospel of Christ. God encourages women to teach, and women need the godly wisdom of older women in order to live in a world that is full of deceit.

Secondly, married women should seek to be involved in ministry with their husbands. Not all couples are called to vocational ministry. In fact, Priscilla and Aquila were tentmakers and not full-time ministers, but they made time to serve God together. God can do powerful and amazing things through a couple who is willing to give Him their time, talents, and marriage in order to further His kingdom. During a time when families are too busy to help in the local church, this couple serves as an example to do ministry wherever you are—whether it is at home, at work, or at church.

If you are married, do you and your husband serve together? If not, what is stopping you?

Explain how you have seen God use couples in ministry—and not necessarily vocational ministers.

What woman in Paul's ministry do you most resonate with? Why?

Wow! We have come to the end of our journey together. My prayer is that God has shown you more of Himself and His passionate love and affection toward you. Ladies, we all have a ministry God has called us to do, and He has equipped us to do it. Let's not get hung up on what we can't do, which I pray you have seen is very limited, and let's begin celebrating what we are doing. We need each other in ministry. You have gifts and talents that I only dream of possessing, so use them well.

REST STOP: End with a prayer asking God to help you be faithful to the ministry He has called you to do. Dedicate yourself to His plan and purpose for your life.

If God ever gives us a chance to meet, I look forward to hearing your story and how He is using you in His plan. Know you have someone praying for you and cheering you on. Get out there and make Satan shake in his less-than-designer boots. God's got a plan for you, sister! I can't wait to see what it is! I pray that you will embrace God's design for your life, marriage, and ministry. I love you, and I have enjoyed serving alongside you!

Bibliography

Anders, Max. *Galatians–Colossians*. Holman New Testament Commentary. Vol. 8. Nashville: Broadman & Holman, 1999.

Belleville, Linda L. "Women in Ministry: An Egalitarian Perspective." In *Two Views on Women in Ministry*, ed. James R. Beck, 19–104. Grand Rapids, MI: Zondervan, 2005.

_____. "Women Leaders in the Bible." In *Discovering Biblical Equality: Complementarity without Hierarchy*, ed. Ronald W. Pierce and Rebecca Merrill Groothuis, 110–125. Downers Grove, IL: InterVarsity, 2005.

"Betty Friedan Biography." *Encyclopedia of World Biography* [online]. Accessed September 12, 2012; available from http:// www.notablebiographies.com/FiGi/Friedan-Betty.html; Internet.

Bilezikian, Gilbert. *Beyond Sex Roles: What the Bible Says about a Woman's Place in Church and Family*. 2nd ed. Grand Rapids, MI: Baker, 1985.

_____, Stanley N. Gundry, Catherine Clark Kroeger, Roger Nicole, *et al. Men, Women and Biblical Equality*. Minneapolis: Christians for Biblical Equality [online PDF].

Accessed September 28, 2012; available from http://www.
cbeinternational.org/sites/default/files/english_0.pdf/;
Internet.

Boa, Kenneth, and William Kruidenier. *Romans*. Holman
New Testament Commentary. Vol. 6. Nashville: Broadman &
Holman, 2000.

Bratcher, Robert G., and Eugene Albert Nida. *A Handbook
on Paul's Letter to the Ephesians*. New York: United Bible
Societies, 1993.

Carson, D. A. "'Silent in the Churches': On the Role of Women
in 1 Corinthians 14:33b–36." In *Recovering Biblical Manhood
and Womanhood: A Response to Evangelical Feminism*,
ed. John Piper and Wayne Grudem, 140–153. Wheaton, IL:
Crossway, 2006.

Erickson, Millard J. *Christian Theology*. Grand Rapids, MI:
Baker, 1983.

Fee, Gordon D. *The First Epistle to the Corinthians*. Grand
Rapids, MI: Eerdmans, 1987.

_____. "Praying and Prophesying in the Assemblies."
In *Discovering Biblical Equality: Complementarity without
Hierarchy*, ed. Ronald W. Pierce and Rebecca Merrill Groothuis,
142–160. Downers Grove, IL: InterVarsity, 2005.

Finch, Candi. "Women, Pornography, and Our Sexualized
Culture," *Biblical Woman* (blog), *BiblicalWoman.org*, November
8, 2012, accessed January 24, 2015. http://biblicalwoman.com/
women-pornography-and-our-sexualized-culture/

Gangel, Kenneth O. *John*, Holman New Testament Commentary.
Vol. 4. Nashville: Broadman & Holman, 2000.

_____. *Acts*. Holman New Testament Commentary. Vol. 5. Nashville: Broadman & Holman, 1998.

Grenz, Stanley J., and Denise Muir Kjesbo. *Women in the Church: A Biblical Theology of Women in Ministry*. Downers Grove, IL: InterVarsity, 1995.

Grudem, Wayne. *Evangelical Feminism and Biblical Truth: An Analysis of More than 100 Disputed Questions*. Wheaton, IL: Crossway, 2012.

_____. "The Key Issues in the Manhood-Womanhood Controversy, and the Way Forward." In *Biblical Foundations for Manhood and Womanhood*, ed. Wayne Grudem, 19–68. Wheaton, IL: Crossway, 2002.

Henry, Matthew. "Genesis 2:21–25." *Matthew Henry's Commentary on the Whole Bible: Complete Unabridged in One Volume*. Peabody, MA: Hendrickson, 1994.

Kassian, Mary. "Cutting It Straight: The Need for a Sound Hermeneutic." In *Women's Evangelical Commentary: New Testament*, ed. Dorothy Kelley Patterson and Rhonda Harrington Kelley, xxi–xxx. Nashville: Broadman & Holman, 2006.

Kroeger, Richard Clark, and Catherine Clark Kroeger. *I Suffer Not a Woman: Rethinking 1 Timothy 2:11–15 in Light of Ancient Evidence*. Grand Rapids, MI: Baker, 1992.

Larson, Knute. *I & II Thessalonians, I & II Timothy, Titus, Philemon*. Vol. 9. Holman New Testament Commentary. Nashville: Broadman & Holman, 2000.

Lea, Thomas D., and Hayne P. Griffin. *1, 2 Timothy, Titus*. New American Commentary. Vol. 34. Nashville: Broadman & Holman, 1992.

MacArthur, John. *First Corinthians*. MacArthur New Testament Commentary. Chicago: Moody Press, 1984.

_____. *1 Timothy*. MacArthur New Testament Commentary. Chicago: Moody Press, 1995.

Mathews, K. A. *Genesis 1–11:26*. New American Commentary. Vol. 1. Nashville: Broadman & Holman, 1996.

Moore, Beth. *So long Insecurity: You've Been a Bad Friend to Us*. Carol Stream, IL: Tyndale House, 2010.

Mussett, Shannon. "Simone de Beauvoir." *Internet Encyclopedia of Philosophy*. Utah Valley University, 2010 [online]. Accessed 15 February 2013; available from www. iep.utm.edu/beauvoir/#SH3a; Internet.

Patterson, Dorothy Kelley. "The High Calling of Wife and Mother in Biblical Perspective." In *Recovering Biblical Manhood and Womanhood: A Response to Evangelical Feminism*, eds. John Piper and Wayne Grudem. Wheaton, IL: Crossway, 2006.

Patterson, Dorothy Kelley, and Rhonda Harrington Kelley, eds. *Women's Evangelical Commentary: New Testament*. Nashville: Broadman & Holman, 2006.

_____., eds. *Women's Evangelical Commentary: Old Testament*. Nashville: Broadman and Holman, 2011.

Pierce, Ronald W. "From Old Testament Law to New Testament Gospel." In *Discovering Biblical Equality: Complementarity without Hierarchy*, ed. Ronald W. Pierce and Rebecca Merrill Groothuis, 96–109. Downers Grover, IL: InterVarsity, 2005.

Pratt, Richard L., Jr. *I and II Corinthians*. Holman New Testament Commentary. Vol. 7. Nashville: Broadman & Holman, 2000.

Ryrie, Charles. *The Role of Women in the Church*. Nashville: Broadman & Holman, 2011.

Schreiner, Thomas R. "Head Coverings, Prophecies, and the Trinity: 1 Corinthians 11:2–16." In *Recovering Biblical Manhood and Womanhood: A Response to Evangelical Feminism*, ed. John Piper and Wayne Grudem, 124–139. Wheaton, IL: Crossway, 2006.

_____. "The Valuable Ministries of Women in the Context of Male Leadership: A Survey of Old and New Testament Examples and Teaching." In *Rediscovering Biblical Manhood and Womanhood: A Response to Evangelical Feminism*, ed. John Piper and Wayne Grudem, 209–224. Wheaton, IL: Crossway, 2006.

Spencer, Aída Besançon. *Beyond the Curse: Women Called to Ministry*. Grand Rapids: Baker Academic, 1985.

_____. "Jesus' Testament of Women in the Gospels." In *Discovering Biblical Equality: Complementarity without Hierarchy*, ed. Ronald W. Pierce and Rebecca Merrill Groothuis, 126–141. Downers Grove, IL: InterVarsity, 2005.

Strong, James. *A Concise Dictionary of the Words in the Greek Testament and the Hebrew Bible*. Vol. 2. CD-ROM. Bellingham, WA: Logos Bible Software, 2009.

Sumner, Sarah. *Men and Women in the Church: Building Consensus on Christian Leadership.* Downers Grove, IL: InterVarsity, 2003.

Thomas, Robert L. *New American Standard Hebrew-Aramaic and Greek Dictionaries: Updated Edition.* Anaheim, CA: Foundation Publication, 1998.

Thiselton, Anthony C. *The First Epistle to the Corinthians: A Commentary on the Greek Text.* New International Greek Testament Commentary. Grand Rapids, MI: Eerdmans, 2000.

Utley, Robert James. *Paul's Letters to a Troubled Church: I and II Corinthians.* Study Guide Commentary Series. Vol. 6. Marshall, TX: Bible Lessons International, 2002.

Wuest, Kenneth S. *Wuest's Word Studies from the Greek New Testament: For the English Reader.* Grand Rapids, MI: Eerdmans, 1997.

Week 1: The Journey Begins: Understanding God's Design

1. Millard J. Erickson, *Christian Theology* (Grand Rapids: Baker Book House, 1983), 21.
2. Gilbert Bilezikian, Stanley N. Gundry, Catherine Clark Kroger, Roger Nicole, et. al. *Men, Women, and Biblical Equality* (Minneapolis: Christians for Biblical Equality), accessed 28 September 2012; available from http://www.cbeinternational.org/sites/default/files/english_0.pdf. These authors write from the egalitarian position of manhood and womanhood.
3. Go to *The Counsel on Biblical Manhood and Womanhood* at www.cbmw.org for more information on the complementarian position of manhood and womanhood.
4. Dorothy Kelley Patterson and Rhonda Harrington Kelley, eds., *Women's Evangelical Commentary: Old Testament* (Nashville: Broadman and Holman, 2011), 5. The authors in this commentary write from a complementarian position of manhood and womanhood.
5. K. A. Mathews, *Genesis 1–11:26*. The New American Commentary, vol. 1 (Nashville: Broadman & Holman, 1996), 218.
6. Matthew Henry, *Matthew Henry's Commentary on the Whole Bible: Complete Unabridged in One Volume* (Peabody: Hendrickson, 1994), Genesis 2:21–25.
7. In Genesis 1:29, God commands the man and woman to only eat from the plants and trees. Man did not have permission to eat of the animals until after the Fall (see Genesis 3:9).

8   Robert L. Thomas, *New American Standard Hebrew-Aramaic and Greek Dictionaries: Updated Edition* (Anaheim: Foundation Publication, 1998). Word study of the Hebrew word *shamar*, Strong's Hebrew #8104.

9   Matthews, *Genesis 1–11:26*, 209–210.

10 Wayne Grudem, *Evangelical Feminism and Biblical Truth* (Wheaton, IL: Crossway, 2012), 31. For a more thorough understanding of the authority that is found in naming an object or individual, refer to pages 31–33 of this volume.

11 Bilezikian, *Beyond Sex Roles*, 259.

12 Beth Moore, *So Long Insecurity: You've Been a Bad Friend to Us* (Carol Stream, IL: Tyndale House, 2010), 186–188.

13 Patterson and Kelley, *Woman's Evangelical Commentary: Old Testament*, 10.

Week 2: The Detour: What Went Wrong?

14 K. A. Matthews, *Genesis 1–11:26*. The New American Commentary, vol. 1 (Nashville: Broadman & Holman, 1996), 244.

15 Dorothy Kelley Patterson and Rhonda Harrington Kelley, eds., *Women's Evangelical Commentary: Old Testament* (Nashville: Broadman & Holman, 2011), 15.

16 James Strong, *A Concise Dictionary of the Words in the Greek Testament and the Hebrew Bible*, (Bellingham: Logos Bible Software, 2009), Vol. 2, 115.

17 Patterson and Kelley, *Woman's Evangelical Commentary: Old Testament*, 16–17.

18 Wayne Grudem, "The Key Issues in the Manhood-Womanhood Controversy, and the Way Forward" in *Biblical Foundations for Manhood and Womanhood* (Wheaton, IL: Crossway, 2002), 34.

19 Shannon Mussett, "Simone de Beauvoir." *Internet Encyclopedia of Philosophy* (Utah Valley University, 2010) [online]; accessed 15 February 2013; available from www.iep.utm.edu/beauvoir/#SH3a; Internet.

20 *Encyclopedia of World Biography*, "Betty Friedan Biography" [online]; accessed 6 September 2012; available from www.notablebiographies.com/Fi-Gi/Friedan-Betty.html; Internet.

Week 3: Getting Back on Track: God's Design for Marriage

[21] Max Anders, *Galatians–Colossians*. Holman New Testament Commentary, Vol. 8 (Nashville: Broadman and Holman, 1999), 275. The author of this commentary writes from a complementarian position of manhood and womanhood.

[22] Dorothy Kelley Patterson and Rhonda Harrington Kelley, eds., *Women's Evangelical Commentary: New Testament* (Nashville: Broadman and Holman, 2006), 564–565. The authors in this commentary write from a complementarian position of manhood and womanhood.

[23] Robert L. Thomas, *New American Standard Hebrew–Aramaic and Greek Dictionaries: Updated Edition* (Anaheim: Foundation Publications, 1998), Strong's number 5293.

[24] Patterson and Kelley, *Women's Evangelical Commentary: New Testament*, 561.

[25] Robert G. Bratcher and Eugene Albert Nida, *A Handbook on Paul's Letter to the Ephesians* (New York: United Bible Societies, 1993), 139.

[26] Kenneth S. Wuest, *Wuest's Word Studies from the Greek New Testament: For the English Reader* (Grand Rapids: Eerdmans, 1997). Word study on Ephesians 5:25–27, especially focusing on the word "love."

[27] Anders, 175.

[28] Anders, 566.

Week 4: The Road Map for Discipleship: The Titus 2 Woman

[29] Dorothy Kelley Patterson and Rhonda Harrington Kelley, eds., *Women's Evangelical Commentary: New Testament* (Nashville: Broadman and Holman, 2006), 732.

[30] Patterson and Kelley, 732.

[31] Patterson and Kelley, 732.

[32] Knute Larson, *1 & 2 Thessalonians, 1 & 2 Timothy, Titus, Philemon*, Holman New Testament Commentary, Vol. 9, (Nashville: Broadman and Holman, 2000), 360.

[33] Larson, 361.

[34] Patterson and Kelley, 735.

[35] Candi Finch, "Women, Pornography, and Our Sexualized Culture," *Biblical Woman* (blog), *BiblicalWoman.org*, November

8, 2012, accessed January 24, 2015. http://biblicalwoman.com/women-pornography-and-our-sexualized-culture/

36 Dorothy Patterson, "The High Calling of Wife and Mother in Biblical Perspective," in *Recovering Biblical Manhood and Womanhood: A Response to Evangelical Feminism*, eds. John Piper and Wayne Grudem (Wheaton: Crossway, 2006), 365. This article is written from a complementarian view of manhood and womanhood.

37 Larson, 362.

38 Patterson and Kelley, 736.

Week 5: Drivers Beware: Interpreting Difficult Passages

39 Mary A. Kassian, "Cutting It Straight: The Need for a Sound Hermeneutic," in *Women's Evangelical Commentary: New Testament*, eds. Dorothy Kelley Patterson and Rhonda Harrington Kelley (Nashville: Broadman and Holman, 2006), xxii.

40 Kassian, xxiii-xxiv.

41 Dorothy Kelley Patterson and Rhonda Harrington Kelley, eds., *Women's Evangelical Commentary: New Testament* (Nashville: Broadman and Holman, 2006), 457–458.

42 Anothony C. Thiselton, *The First Epistle to the Corinthians*, 1148. The original source for this statement is in Gordon D. Fee, *The First Epistle to the Corinthians* (Grand Rapids: Eerdmans, 1987). Fee writes from an egalitarian position of manhood and womanhood.

43 D. A. Carson, "Silent in the Churches: On the Role of Women in 1 Corinthians 14:33b–36," in *Recovering Biblical Manhood and Womanhood: A Response to Evangelical Feminism*, eds. John Piper and Wayne Grudem (Wheaton: Crossway, 2006), 141–142. This article is written from a complementarian position of manhood and womanhood.

44 Robert James Utley, Vol. 6, *Paul's Letters to a Troubled Church: I and II Corinthians*, Study Guide Commentary Series (Marshall: Bible Lessons International, 2002), 166–167.

45 Wayne Grudem, *Evangelical Feminism & Biblical Truth: An Analysis of More Than 100 Disputed Questions* (Wheaton: Crossway, 2012), 243. This author writes from a complementarian position of manhood and womanhood.

46 Carson, 151.

47 These words are used in the KJV and the NASB translations of the Bible.

[48] Carson, 152.

[49] Richard L. Pratt Jr., Vol. 7 *I and II Corinthians*, Holman New Testament Commentary (Nashville: Broadman and Holman, 2000), 250.

[50] Carson, 153.

[51] Grudem, 228–231. For a rebuttal against teaching holding more influence than prophesy, see Aída Besançon Spencer, *Beyond the Curse: Women Called to Ministry* (Grand Rapids: Baker, 1985), 103–108. Her stance is that prophets served like the modern-day preacher. But if you look at 1 Corinthians 14, this stance has problems. One prophesied only when a revelation had come upon him or her, which was a spontaneous act. Preaching in the New Testament is linked to proclaiming the gospel of Jesus Christ, which all believers are called to do.

[52] Charles Ryrie, *The Role of Women in the Church* (Nashville: Broadman and Holman, 2011), 120–127. His explanation of Paul's appeal to the Law is excellent. He has a different view of 1 Corinthians 14:34–35 than is presented, which is beneficial to read. This author writes from a complementarian view of biblical manhood and womanhood.

[53] There are several valid interpretations of 1 Corinthians 14:34–35 that differ from my view. I can only present the material and give what I believe to be the best interpretation of the material. If you have more questions concerning this subject, the provided endnotes will assist you in your research.

[54] Richard Clark Kroeger and Catherine Clark Kroeger, *I Suffer Not a Woman: Rethinking 1 Timothy 2:11–15 in Light of Ancient Evidence* (Grand Rapids: Baker, 1992), 14. These authors write from an egalitarian position of manhood and womanhood.

[55] Kroeger, 103.

[56] Kroeger, 84.

[57] Kroeger, 103.

[58] Kroeger, 103.

[59] Grudem, 281.

[60] Grudem, 284–286.

[61] Gilbert Bilezikian, *Beyond Sex Roles: What the Bible Says about a Woman's Place in Church and Family* (Grand Rapids: Baker, 1985), 180–181. This author writes from an egalitarian position of manhood and womanhood.

[62] Bilezikian, 180.

[63] Grudem, 288–293.

[64] I make this statement because there are arguments from scholars like Richard Clark Kroeger and Catherine Clark Kroeger, *I Suffer Not a*

Woman: Rethinking 1 Timothy 2:11–15 in Light of Ancient Evidence (Grand Rapids: Baker, 1992) who give examples of women who have positions of leadership outside the church. These women have been hurt by this passage, and rightly so. They give these examples in order to show how foolish this passage sounds to the modern Christian.

65   Patterson and Kelley, 664.

66   Thomas D. Lea and Hayne P. Griffin, Vol. 34, *1, 2, Timothy, Titus*, The New American Commentary (Nashville: Broadman and Holman, 1992), 98.

67   Lea and Griffin, 99. Egalitarian scholars like Sarah Sumner, *Men and Women in the Church* (Downers Grove: InterVarsity, 2003) use this example of the Greek verb tense to prove that Paul did mean that women, in every situation, were not to not teach men. Instead, their view is that women in this particular situation were not to "teach or exercise authority over men." Sumner goes on to give instances where Priscilla, a member of the church of Ephesus, taught Apollos.

68   John MacArthur, *The MacArthur New Testament Commentary, 1 Timothy* (Chicago: Moody Press, 1995), 85–89. This author writes from a complementary position of manhood and womanhood.

69   For a more thorough understanding of this view, consider Wayne Grudem, "Prophesy-Yes, But Teaching-No: Paul's Consistent Advocacy of Women's Participation without Governing Authority" in *Journal of the Evangelical Theological Society*, March 1987, 11–23. You can find a copy online at http://www.etsjets.org/files/JETS-PDFs/30/30-1/30-1-pp011-023_JETS.pdf

70   Lea and Griffin, *1, 2 Timothy, Titus*, 99.

71   I have given the example of Apollos learning from Priscilla in Acts 18:26. But, Paul also commends Timothy's mother, Eunice, and grandmother, Lois, who taught him in the faith (2 Tim. 1:5).

72   Thomas R. Schreiner, "Head Coverings, Prophecies, and the Trinity: 1 Corinthians 11:2–16" in *Recovering Biblical Manhood and Womanhood: A Response to Evangelical Feminism*, eds. John Piper and Wayne Grudem (Wheaton: Crossway, 2006), 125–126. This article is written from a complementarian position of manhood and womanhood.

73   Patterson and Kelley, 442.

74   John MacArthur, *The MacArthur New Testament Commentary, 1 Corinthians* (Chicago: Moody Press, 1984), 257–258. This author writes from a complementarian position of manhood and womanhood.

75   Gordon D. Fee, "Praying and Prophesying in the Assemblies" in *Discovering Biblical Equality: Complementarity without Hierarchy*,

eds. Ronald W. Pierce and Rebecca Merrill Groothuis (Downers Grove: InterVarsity, 2005), 152. This author writes from an egalitarian position of manhood and womanhood.

76 Schreiner, 128.
77 Schreiner, 130–131.
78 Grudem, 334–335.
79 MacArthur, *1 Corinthians*, 258–259.
80 Grudem, 336–337.

Week 6: The Destination: Women Celebrated in Ministry

81 Dorothy Kelley Patterson and Rhonda Harrington Kelley, eds., *Women's Evangelical Commentary: New Testament* (Nashville: Broadman and Holman, 2006), 1–2.
82 Patterson and Kelley, 1–2.
83 Ronald W. Pierce, "From Old Testament Law to New Testament Gospel," in *Discovering Biblical Equality: Complementarity without Hierarchy*, eds. Ronald W. Pierce and Rebecca Merrill Groothuis (Downers Grover: InterVarsity, 2005), 97–101. Though this volume is written from an egalitarian position of manhood and womanhood, this section on the Mosaic laws is useful in explaining the protection God gave women under the Law.
84 Patterson and Kelley, 98.
85 Kenneth O. Gangel, Vol. 4, *John*, Holman New Testament Commentary (Nashville: Broadman and Holman, 2000), 74.
86 Gangel, 76.
87 Aída Besançon Spencer, "Jesus' Testament of Women in the Gospels" in *Discovering Biblical Equality: Complementarity without Hierarchy*, eds. Ronald W. Pierce and Rebecca Merrill Groothuis (Downers Grove: InterVarsity, 2005), 134–140.
88 Patterson and Kelley, 186.
89 Kenneth O. Gangel, Vol. 5, *Acts*, Holman New Testament Commentary (Nashville, Broadman and Holman, 1998), 270.
90 Patterson and Kelley, 317.
91 Gangel, *Acts*, 271.
92 Stanley J. Grenz and Denise Muir Kjesbo, *Women in the Church: A Biblical Theology of Women in Ministry* (Downers Grove: InterVarsity, 1995), 77–82. These authors write from an egalitarian position of manhood and womanhood.

93 Kenneth Boa and William Kruidenier, Vol. 6, *Romans*, Holman New Testament Commentary (Nashville: Broadman and Holman, 2000), 458.

94 Kenneth S. Wuest, *Wuest's Word Studies from the Greek New Testament: For the English Reader* (Grand Rapids: Eerdmans, 1997). Word study on Romans 16:1, especially focusing on the word "servant or deaconess."

95 Patterson and Kelley, 406.

96 Boa and Kruidenier, *Romans*, 458.

97 Grenz and Kjesbo, 88–89.

98 Linda L. Belleville, "Women Leaders in the Bible" in *Discovering Biblical Equality: Complementarity without Hierarchy*, eds. Ronald W. Pierce and Rebecca Merrill Groothuis (Downers Grove: InterVarsity, 2005), 120–121.

99 Sarah Sumner, *Men and Women in the Church* (Downers Grove: InterVarsity, 2003), 242–244. This author writes from an egalitarian position of manhood and womanhood.

100 Grenz and Kjesbo, 82–83.

101 Linda L. Belleville, "Women in Ministry: An Egalitarian Perspective" in *Two Views on Women in Ministry*, ed. James R. Beck (Grand Rapids: Zondervan, 2005), 58–59.

102 Thomas R. Schreiner, "The Valuable Ministries of Women in the Context of Male Leadership: A Survey of Old and New Testament Examples and Teaching" in *Rediscovering Biblical Manhood and Womanhood: A Response to Evangelical Feminism*, eds. John Piper and Wayne Grudem (Wheaton: Crossway, 2006), 218–219. This article is written from a complementarian position of manhood and womanhood.

103 Wayne Grudem, *Evangelical Feminism & Biblical Truth: An Analysis of More Than 100 Disputed Questions* (Wheaton: Crossway, 2012), 178–179. This is written from a complementarian position of manhood and womanhood.

CPSIA information can be obtained
at www.ICGtesting.com
Printed in the USA
LVHW04s2235100918
589761LV00001B/189/P